Managing Your Library Construction Project

A STEP-BY-STEP GUIDE

Richard C. McCarthy, AIA

American Library Association

Chicago   2007

While extensive effort has gone into ensuring the reliability of information appearing in this book, the publisher makes no warranty, express or implied, on the accuracy or reliability of the information, and does not assume and hereby disclaims any liability to any person for any loss or damage caused by errors or omissions in this publication.

Published in previous editions by Highsmith Press as *Designing Better Libraries: Selecting and Working with Building Professionals.*

The paper used in this publication meets the minimum requirements of American National Standard for Information Sciences—Permanence of Paper for Printed Library Materials, ANSI Z39.48-1992. ∞

Library of Congress Cataloging-in-Publication Data
McCarthy, Richard C. (Richard Charles), 1955–
    Managing your library construction project : a step-by-step guide / Richard C. McCarthy.
      p. cm.
    "Published in previous editions by Highsmith Press as Designing better libraries : selecting and working with building professionals"—T.p. verso.
    Includes bibliographical references and index.
    ISBN-13: 978-0-8389-0931-7 (alk. paper)
    ISBN-10: 0-8389-0931-0 (alk. paper)
    1. Library buildings—United States—Design and construction.   I. McCarthy, Richard C. (Richard Charles), 1955– Designing better libraries. II. Title.
    Z679.2.U54M33 2007
    727'.8'0973—dc22   2006039317

ISBN-10: 0-8389-0931-0
ISBN-13: 978-0-8389-0931-7

Printed in the United States of America
11 10 09 08 07   5 4 3 2 1

This book is dedicated to my daughter, Mary Augusta McCarthy.

Special thanks to
my wife Susan Stillinger for her unfailing support, and
Miriam Pollack for the idea that led to the writing of this book.

Contents

A Common Language

In architecture school I was taught many things. I learned how to design buildings and how to draw. I learned how a structure stands against the force of gravity and resists attacks by the elements. There were courses in plumbing, electrical systems, and the mechanical properties of soils. We students spent long nights memorizing slides and photographs of significant buildings in architectural history. There was even a one-semester class on office practice, in which the teachers introduced us to the more pragmatic sides of the architectural profession: things like contracts, budgets, liability insurance, and bookkeeping. Being young, we mounted fierce resistance to all things practical and eagerly quit that classroom to return to the design studio where our interests and, we hoped, our talents lay. We spent six years learning the skills and nomenclature of our profession: the art and process of designing buildings. Architecture is one of the few professions that still requires a period of formal apprenticeship. After receiving a degree, the graduate is required to work several years under the tutelage of a licensed architect before he or she can begin the rigorous examination process that is a prerequisite to licensure. In most cases, nine years of a person's life have been devoted to studying the profession before he or she can assume the title of "architect."

Learning the Ropes

Despite its rigors, nothing in our education prepared us to stand up in front of skeptical trustees to try to persuade them of the necessity to spend additional money for their project because the contractor's bids were higher than we had anticipated. There was no training to ready us for difficult negotiations with local authorities to obtain a politically unpopular zoning change on behalf of a client. The problem of nonpayment for services rendered never came up. As is the case with many professions, we learned many of the most important skills of our profession on the job.

Most library board members are elected or appointed to the position without the benefit of years of preparation or a formal training period. Learning the ropes is as important for a new board member as it is for a fledgling architect. New board members find themselves suddenly in the position of having to vote on issues that they may only partially understand. The first board meetings are filled with acronyms that leave novices in a state of confusion. They can be seen furtively searching the board information packet for anything that will help with translation. Budgets are reviewed and at least a passing acquaintance with accountancy is assumed. Library employees who may have formerly been cool and businesslike suddenly seem eager to please. New members are faced with the unfamiliar and an overload of information.

In time, the footing becomes surer. Acronyms begin to assume meaning. With assistance from the more senior members, neophytes begin to feel that they are a part of the group. If the chemistry is right, the board functions as a team, with each member contributing the benefits of personal talents and experience. Sometimes a board is confronted with a problem that lies beyond the combined experience of the group. The decision to construct a new building, or to enlarge an existing one, is not one that needs to be made on a regular basis. Often the last such project predates the terms of the current board members, often even that of the library director.

The degree of success of such an enterprise depends on decisions made early in the project. Its outcome may have an effect on the community for a generation or more. Public bodies often begin this decision-making process not really speaking the same language as the professionals they are proposing to hire, without having a clear idea of the services they need or even of what services are available. Unfortunately, there are no practice runs and few manuals to offer guidance. The learning curve is very steep. In most cases you do it once, and either things turn out as you hoped or they fall short of your expectations.

Thousands of buildings go up each year that are of doubtful aesthetic value but still plod along, functioning pretty much as they were intended. Others sacrifice utility in order to make an artistic statement. Neither of these constitutes an unsuccessful project if the clients got what they wanted and understood in advance the limitations of the finished product. The mission of the architect is to produce the most successful building possible while responding to the varied, and sometimes contradictory, wishes of the client. It is the unpleasant surprises that can cause dissatisfaction with the final result. To avoid these surprises it is important that the client and architect understand each other's language.

Language Lessons

Good architects keep the client fully informed at every step of the project. They spend large amounts of time with the client, explaining the process and progress of the work. Good clients spend the time it takes to keep current with the project. When the client is a group of persons rather than an individual, communication becomes more difficult. Often a board of directors sees the architect only during a project report at a monthly board meeting. Other information about the job comes from intermediaries, perhaps the library director or another staff member. In these instances it is important that each member of the decision-making body have a basic understanding of the process. A book cannot keep you informed of the progress of your particular project, but it can give you an overview of how to work with an architect and of the ways buildings are designed, bid, and built. Understanding the language and methods of the architect enables you to communicate more effectively with each other and thus allows you an active and essential role in the project.

In this book I describe the process of a building project. I take the point of view of an architect—but tempered by the fact that, as of this writing, I am serving my eighteenth year as a library trustee. I try to balance these two roles and present you with as objective a view as is possible. We look at methods that can be used by library boards and directors to aid them in selecting, hiring, and working with architects and other design professionals. I cover what you can expect from an architect in terms of services, offer assistance to help you determine what services you need, and provide examples of documents and graphic presentations. Subjects covered include the parts of a typical architectural project, the evaluation of architectural firms, guidelines for interviewing architects, and advice on coping with common problems and procedures during construction. An understanding of the process boosts the chances of a successful project and helps ensure that you get your money's worth for the professional services for which you pay.

I do not attempt to offer more than the most general guidelines for designing libraries. There are several guides in print that propose standards for public libraries. Some of these documents are listed in the bibliography at the end of this book. Standards such as these should be used by the client, the library building consultant, and the architect to arrive at a design solution appropriate to the particular circumstances. I recommend that you examine such materials before beginning a project.

With all the responsibilities of spending the public's money on a complex undertaking, you may feel that the weight of the world is on your shoulders. Take advantage of this opportunity to have some fun! In a well-run project, all participants have a part in the creative effort. The architect brings focus to the endeavor, but you are in control. This is the time for you to express your hopes and ideas and see them realized in the form of a building. I find that learning about my clients is the most rewarding part of my profession. As an architect, I have a unique opportunity to step into their shoes, to see how they live and work and to help them seek solutions to their problems. For the client, this is a time of self-examination. You learn a lot about yourself and about how your library functions. This is the time for you to step back and take an objective look at how you do things. The opportunity to change the built environment may bring the chance to improve your operations. Encourage staff involvement in this appraisal process and invite their input at every opportunity. There are all sorts of good ideas out there that are just waiting to be heard.

Chapter 1

First Things First

There are several questions you should ask yourself before considering a building project. The first and most obvious is best summed up by an old poster from World War II. The poster was intended to promote gasoline rationing and showed a stylish woman driving a convertible along a picturesque rural road, picnic supplies sitting on the back seat. The message at the bottom of the poster asks, "Is this trip really necessary?" I suspect that most readers have already persuaded themselves that it is, but the issue still merits some thought. Your reasons for a construction project must be put forth in a clear and concise form, both as a basis for internal discussion and to provide justification required by the tax-paying public or other funding sources. Alternatives to new construction should always be considered. When the financial state of the library is less than robust, working within the existing structure may be your only option. Some preliminary work is required for this kind of analysis.

Consider Your Alternatives

The alternatives to a new building or addition are often far less exciting than the idea of building something new. Remodeling just doesn't capture one's imagination in the same way. An "Excuse our dust!" sign in the lobby can seem like a poor substitute for a newspaper photo of a groundbreaking. But if a shortage of space is the main problem, stacks, reading tables, card catalogs, and the like can often be rearranged in a more efficient manner. An unused basement space might be finished and utilized as a public area. In a real pinch, mobile units may be brought in (on a temporary basis, we hope) for storage or staff space. An architect can help you evaluate these options and provide alternate plans and budget figures. Since the passage of the Americans with Disabilities Act (ADA), some interior improvements trigger additional work, sometimes undermining the rationale of these cost-saving alternatives. Program changes can also be considered. Things the library currently provides that may be considered secondary services, like meeting rooms or specialized collections, could be sacrificed to free up space for primary services. Triage of library services should be reserved for real emergencies, for the results can easily be counterproductive in terms of public opinion.

The Best of Intentions versus Unintended Consequences

On occasion, the quest for improved library services can have unintended consequences. We are routinely hired by libraries to help them deal with cramped, overcrowded conditions in existing structures. Our client's goal is usually to increase the efficiency of the library, open up the interior, and provide an overall impression more in keeping with the public's impression of how a twenty-first-century library should look and function.

Many older libraries have expanded "organically," making incremental changes to deal with new challenges as they arose. Examples of organic expansion include shoehorning in additional stacks to accommodate growing collections, squeezing additional staff offices into previously unused corners or needed storage spaces, sacrificing meeting rooms for collection space, and utilizing the top and bottom shelves of the existing stacks. Here is where those unintended consequences might appear. We often find that bringing libraries that have expanded in an organic fashion in line with current, accepted standards of library design would actually reduce the size of the collection. A simple example is shelf spacing; we have run into libraries which, as a result of growth, have been left with aisles of barely 30 inches. Bringing such a library into conformance with the ADA would increase the spacing between the shelves and probably reduce the size of the collection if we are working within an existing building. It's an uncomfortable position; we were hired to make the library more efficient and increase the size of the collection, yet we must bring our client the unhappy news that the collection should be decreased. Faced with this situation, some clients that have other, larger libraries within a reasonable distance opt to change the emphasis of their collection, reducing it to handle what they can actually house. Some, for example, cede serious research materials to the larger libraries and orient their own collections toward popular materials and electronic resources.

Other considerations conspire against the case for remodeling. A current bogeyman in the world of building restoration is asbestos. If your building was built before the early 1970s, it is likely that it contains many forms of this versatile, and now prohibited, material. In many of its applications, asbestos is a relatively innocuous substance. It resides in boiler rooms and above ceilings, quietly fireproofing structural steel and insulating pipes. It replaced horsehair as an ingredient in plaster. In older floor tiles it is a binder, holding the tiles together to ensure a long-wearing floor. Try to alter any of these installations, however, and Pandora's box is opened. You no doubt already know that disturbing asbestos can release large numbers of the carcinogenic fibers into the air; this is prohibited by federal law. The legal alternative is often to release large sums of your money into the pocket of an asbestos abatement contractor. Removing asbestos can be expensive. Costs for the management of asbestos and other environmental issues should always be researched and considered in a remodeling project.

Having a historically significant building for your library is often something between a mixed blessing and a disaster if you are considering alterations. Structures on the National Register of Historic Buildings are protected by state and federal regulations that limit the kinds of alteration that may be made. Most states have a central office for the National Register. You or your architect should contact this office before contemplating any changes to a listed building.

State Your Case

Whether you can sell the concept of remodeling or of new construction to those who will eventually foot the bill depends on how well they understand the need for the project. This seems obvious, and indeed it is. Every year, however, referenda are lost, grant proposals are rejected, and city councils are not persuaded because someone didn't prepare the way. Communicating the necessity for your project is vitally important.

Some of the reasons that make you consider remodeling or building are evident to the public, and some are not. Even a severe shortage of space, one of the most basic reasons for a construction project, may not be apparent to the average library user. People don't expect to see a lot of empty space on library shelves. They may take some note when the books are jammed together so tightly that they become difficult to remove, but they probably won't notice that the collection is being severely weeded just to make room for even a minimum number of new acquisitions.

The sitting areas may have steadily shrunk before the glacial advance of the stacks, but most of the time most patrons can still find a seat. But those patrons seldom get to see the staff areas. Cataloging and shelving rooms may have books stacked several feet high on every horizontal surface, or there may be eight staffers crammed into a room designed for four. But to the average visitor all seems, if not well, at least adequate.

Aged and inefficient mechanical systems coupled with inadequate building insulation may result in high utility bills, but few beyond the board and the book-keeper know of them. Your present building, especially if it's an older one, may not be accessible to the handicapped. If it isn't, changes are mandated by the ADA. In a multistory structure these changes can become quite costly. If the building already possesses other inherent shortcomings, the extent of the work required to bring it into ADA conformity can be significant.

Making the public aware of your needs is an important and challenging element of any fund-raising effort. Many libraries depend on referenda for capital improvements. This usually means that the library director, board members, and library supporters hit the local lecture circuit. They can be seen stumping for the library, competing with rubber chicken and rice pilaf for the attention of noon-hour Rotarians. On an appointed board it may be possible to select a member or two based primarily on their public image and speaking abilities. In times of need, this can be a good investment.

Some shortcomings are more obvious to the public and much easier to sell. Parking can be a real problem. It is an unfortunate fact that in our society people are unaccustomed to walking. Indeed, the lack of public transportation and the car-centered layouts of our cities often make walking to the library impossible. Public libraries often tend to be located in older, established areas, often down-town. Many downtown plans predate the age of the automobile, so parking can be scarce, inconveniencing those who must drive to the library. A deteriorating neighborhood, another common condition in downtown areas, may cause people to want the library relocated to a "safer" part of town. Basing a decision to move on this reasoning can have important political considerations, for a public library may be the last, best hope for revitalizing a distressed area. There may be a public demand for more amenities such as meeting rooms, or other space for scheduled events. Expanding children's services can be a popular move along with the addition of special collections. At my own library, one of the most popular areas is the genealogy collection. Making this resource available to the public generated more support for funding efforts than any amount of complaining about leaking roofs, old boilers, and worn-out carpet.

Sometimes a structure suffices for the present but falls short in projections of future needs. If the building site is fully utilized and some adjacent property becomes available, a "now or never" decision may be required, always an uncomfortable position for a board member. Persuading someone to spend money based on anticipation of future needs can be difficult. Many libraries have found it helpful to retain specialized consultants to direct and lend credence to their efforts.

Your Team: The Building Committee

Your in-house team is just as important as the team eventually assembled by the architect. An important first step in any project is defining which board and staff members will work most closely with the architect. From the earliest stages of a project, a library should have a building committee to coordinate the efforts of the board and staff. A well-balanced building committee includes several board members, the library director, and several staff members.

The building committee is generally called on for two types of task. In the earliest stages of the project, information gathering is the primary objective. The general focus of such efforts may be set by a building consultant or by an architect, but the responsibility for the collection of information often rests with the staff. Later in the process, decision making becomes more important. At this stage, the board members bear the ultimate responsibility, since many of the decisions involve money and must be approved by the board. The library staff, however, advises the board at this time. Few board members can make a full-time commitment to the project and thus must depend on the director and staff to function as their eyes and ears.

In the case of a public library, I often suggest that the building committee include no more than two board members. There is a simple rationale for this: public meeting requirements are demanding. In many states, any meeting of more than two members of a board of trustees requires that the meeting be "public," that is, advertised in advance, conforming to a published agenda, and open to the public. This suggestion is not a criticism of open government; it is an observation that following all the open meeting requirements for every gathering of the building committee can be unduly restrictive, inefficient, and costly. Under such requirements, quick, informal meetings for late-breaking project issues are impossible and the progress can be impeded by the timing requirements for meeting advertisements.

Having just a few board members sit on a building committee and make their reports to the full board has other advantages. Of course, the first is time. Building projects can require many additional meetings beyond the usual monthly board session. Not all board members may be able to make the commitment for the additional time. More important, when the building committee reports to the full board, the remainder of the board members function as an important check on the committee's recommendations. Decisions of any importance are always best reviewed with fresh insight.

It makes sense to have the director and several department heads represent the staff on a building committee. Other staff members with appropriate talents should also be considered. A lot of information will be funneled through these individuals, and people with good listening and organizational skills are always assets to the committee. Management skills are also a plus. Good internal management helps maintain a smooth flow of information to the design professionals and makes for efficient use of the resources you are paying for. Teamwork is the most essential ingredient of a successful project.

A House Divided

To this point, the project has been defined in only the broadest of terms. The design isn't fixed, and costs are only the roughest of approximations. Even in this framework, however, it is important that there be consensus regarding the need for the work. Is the project, or at least the concept of the project, supported by the entire board?

A library building consultant can help bring a board together. Some states mandate the use of a library building consultant for projects over a specified minimum cost. The consultant makes an in-depth study of the level of service provided by the current facility and evaluates it in terms of present and projected needs. Having an outside consultant confirm what the library director has been saying regarding the inadequacies of the current library can help persuade undecided board members and give the rest of the board a greater level of comfort. Building consultants do not design the new buildings or additions, but they can provide an idea of the approximate floor space required. It is an easy matter to apply the square footage to the average cost of construction in your area and get a rough estimate of the cost of the building. When doing this, it is important to take into account the costs of site work, furnishings, and alterations to the existing structure. They can add a hefty and sometimes unexpected surcharge to the cost of a building. We return to this subject in chapter 14, when we discuss the difference between building costs and project costs.

After the library consultant's report is completed, an architect can be brought in on a preliminary basis to help the board analyze the feasibility of the proposed project. The library can retain an architect to do a feasibility study without committing to this architect for the rest of the project. A feasibility study may also add to the comfort level within the board.

The points above assume that objections to expansion of the library are based on the state of the library's finances. There are, however, other reasons board members may not support a large capital project. There may be differences in philosophy regarding the role of the library in the community. A member may object to the library providing services that don't seem to fall within the traditional role of a library (A/V collections, meeting rooms, public use computers, specialized children's libraries). An elected member on a district board may have run on a "No new taxes" platform or just have a very conservative stand on the expenditure of public money. The best answer for these dilemmas may involve educating the board on the range of services modern libraries offer. Even the most fiscally conservative people can usually be convinced that a library is an investment in the future of their community.

I first ran for our local library board because I love libraries, not because I had a profound understanding of their problems or particular insight into their function in our society. Over time I gained a deeper appreciation of what they can offer and of the challenges facing them in these times of tight money. I believe that the more a person knows about libraries, the more that person is likely to support improvements of all types. Local library systems and state library associations provide many avenues for trustee education. Urge new board members to explore some of these opportunities. Consensus comes more easily in an informed board.

The Longest Journey Begins with a Single Step

That first step is an important one; if taken with assurance and planning, it can set the direction and pace for the largest of projects. If tentative and unprepared, it may set a precedent for indecision. For a library board considering a construction project, the first step is the definition of a goal. Without a goal we cannot define a project, or if need be, defend it. Do you wish merely to reflect the community's growth with proportional expansion at the library? Is the aim to provide a wider range of services to the public, or to enhance certain aspects that might complement those of other local libraries? Do you wish to expand all departments equally, or is the aim to develop an appeal to a special group of library users—say, business people or children? To define your goals, you must consider such questions and adopt decisions formally. The library director brings professional experience in library science, and this should inform the drive behind the formulation of the initial goals. For a library, the goals can be stated in the form of a five-, ten-, or twenty-year plan. This plan is your first step.

The development of a long-range plan is not within the scope of this book. It should be an ongoing process at every library. If your institution lacks a solid long-term plan, or if the existing one is out of date, the development of such a plan should be made a priority. Your state library and local library system can supply materials and consultants to assist the planning efforts.

The Library Building Consultant

With a long-term plan in hand, you are in a position to consider hiring a consultant to analyze your needs and develop a plan that states what is required to satisfy those needs. That consultant may be either an architect or professional library building consultant. As mentioned earlier, some states require use of a library building consultant for projects over a specified size to qualify for public funding. The requirements vary, so you should seek the opinion of your state library before committing to a course of action. Lets look at the difference between library building consultants and architects.

In this book, a library building consultant is a library professional who consults with libraries to help them identify their long-term service goals. This person almost certainly has an MLS and several years' experience in hands-on library work. Many of the building consultants I have worked with are current or retired library directors and possess a wealth of library programming experience.

The scope of services of a library building consultant somewhat overlaps the scope of services traditionally offered by an architect. There are, however, advantages to beginning with a library building consultant rather than an architect:

- Library building consultants usually come from a library background. Some are or have been library directors. In the preface of this book I mentioned the need for a common language. The library building consultant arrives on the scene already fluent in the language of the library professional, which can make the communication between library and architect more efficient. This is especially useful if the architect you eventually select does not have a lot of experience in library design.

- The use of a library building consultant may open up the field of architects you consider for your project, allowing you to expand your options. The program developed by the library building consultant would be a uniform point of beginning for any architect's efforts.

- Drawing on a larger base of library experience, the library building consultant may be better able to anticipate problems and opportunities particular to your library environment.

- The library building consultant may have a better grasp than the average architect of specialized sources of funding for libraries.
- Retaining a library building consultant can lend credibility to the planning effort. Political realities may demand that advice regarding the expenditure of public money come from a "disinterested" source. A library building consultant who has no vested interest in the outcome of the planning process can be that disinterested third party.

What should you expect from your library building consultant? In short, a library building consultant produces a building program. I discuss just what a building program should include in chapter 4. For the moment, suffice it to say that a building program defines every space or use in the proposed building and assigns each an approximate square footage. Furniture and equipment requirements are itemized, and how the room must relate to the spaces around it is discussed. The square footage figures can be used for a first intimation of the cost of your project. Note that the library building consultant's report does not generally take financial considerations into account. It is intended to assess needs independent of the means required to meet those needs.

The Financial Planning Consultant

How much money do you have? How much do you spend? How much are you going to have? How much are you going to need? Unfortunately, we do have to ask, but it may turn out to be affordable—contrary to Morgan's classic line. The real question is *how* to afford it, and this question is important in your planning process. An expert third-party evaluation of your current financial state and prospects for the future is an important component of a long-range plan. When seeking additional funding for your institution, be it by grant, appropriation, or referendum, this kind of expert opinion is advisable and may be mandatory. There is (not surprisingly) another consultant in the lineup who specializes in just these kinds of evaluations: the financial planning consultant.

The library building consultant's report gives you an idea of the size of your project. In many cases the architect is retained around this time to turn the estimated square footage into an initial cost estimate for your library. At this point you are ready to begin talking to a financial planning consultant, who can assist you in three general areas: the financial plan, referenda, procuring investments.

The Financial Plan

The financial plan is a necessary companion to the long-range plan. The financial plan takes into account all aspects of the library's present and anticipated financial condition. Like the long-range plan, the financial plan may be written with a ten- to twenty-year horizon. After comparing anticipated revenue with projected expenditures, this study adds inflation to the mix, and a projection of the long-term financial condition of the library emerges. Many of these numbers are necessarily based on educated guesses. Projecting the library's income may require predicting future tax rates, the political climate, and changes in assessed valuation. An accurate estimate of future expenses also requires that the crystal ball be tuned to the rate of inflation and general trends in library services. Finally, a healthy amount of contingency is added to the equation to cover unforeseen developments. It would

If you have to ask, you can't afford it.

—J. P. Morgan

be an interesting exercise to look at some twenty-year-old financial plans to see if any of them correctly predicted the costs of the computers and associated technologies that are so prominent in contemporary libraries.

Like the library building consultant, the financial planning consultant works closely with the library director to formulate evaluations. The board is most likely only peripherally involved until the presentation of the financial plan. When the financial report is presented, it gives solid information on the means and methods of implementing the long-term plan, including proposed changes or additions to the library. It establishes the tax rates required to implement plans, indicates whether a referendum will be required, and, if so, can specify the types of questions needed on the ballot. For libraries not fueled by tax dollars, it can advise about the amounts and sources of funding needed.

Taking It to the Voters

Referenda are unpredictable. Like children, no two of them are alike. Strategies that bring success in one situation may flop in another. Many board members have little experience launching a referendum campaign. It therefore makes sense to take advantage of any expertise at your disposal for such an important effort. Many financial planning consultants can also offer assistance with your campaign. The amount of help they can provide varies widely depending on your needs and in-house abilities.

Financial planning consultants can assist many aspects of running a referendum campaign. They may help determine the overall strategy for a campaign or assist in any of a hundred small details that can make the difference between winning and losing. Techniques for informing the voters, election timing, coordination of publicity, and formulation of citizens' committees may be included. A strong citizens' committee adds many voices to your cause; the more voters involved, the better the chances of success. The right financial planning consultant knows ways to promote strong public involvement in an effort.

In addition to the financial planning consultant, the state library and local library system can be important sources of help and information. They often have collections of referenda materials distributed by other libraries in your state and records of past voting results that you can use in your planning.

Procuring Investments

After a successful referendum, the financial planning consultant can direct the sale and marketing of general obligation library bonds or mortgage notes, determine the timing of the sale, set the terms, and recommend taking bids for the bond registrar, printer, and counsel. Finally, the consultant can recommend that the sale be either negotiated or competitively bid.

After these decisions are made, the consultant writes a prospectus for review by potential investors. General obligation bonds for libraries are usually considered attractive investments and are often sold at favorable rates. To boost the attraction of the bonds, the consultant may recommend that the library secure a bond rating from Moody's Investor Service or Standard and Poors. The library board should be kept informed of the actions of the financial consultant, as should the library's legal counsel.

It can take up to two years from the time you begin planning your referendum campaign to the time the money starts rolling in. Add another year or two to complete a building project. This lead time must always be considered in your intermediate and long-term planning.

Experts, Experts Everywhere: Finding Library Consultants

Finding the right consultant requires some homework. In searching for consultants, begin with your state library and library system, some of which keep lists of qualified individuals. Call other libraries in your area that have held successful referenda or recently completed a building project. You will probably find that some of the same names keep turning up, for the field is not large. It should be relatively easy to build a list of persons to interview. Two publications listed in this book's bibliography can help you interview and hire library consultants: *Selecting Library Consultants,* by Richard Finn and James R. Johnston, and *Building a New Library,* by Anthony J. Batco and Richard E. Thompson. These references are published by the Illinois Library Association as part of its Trustee Facts File, a collection of articles devoted to the education of library trustees. Contact your state library association to see if it publishes similar materials.

Chapter 2

*Architecture is the art
of how to waste space.*

—Philip Johnson

When to Use an Architect

Philip Johnson was a world-famous architect and noted writer of architectural theory. I am therefore ill qualified to comment on his summation of our mutual profession. In spite of this, I will say that I suspect that it would be a grave marketing error to describe oneself as an accomplished waster of space. I also feel obliged to add a few items to his version of our job description. The real question is, What can an architect do for you? In this age of the specialist, most architects still regard themselves as generalists and customarily offer a wide range of services that address nearly anything that involves a building or a site. They are accustomed to familiarizing themselves with the characteristics of many different types of building. In chapter 11 I discuss whether or when it is important to hire an architect with extensive experience designing libraries.

When to Call In the Architect

Most people envision an architect as the designer of buildings. They may have mental images of presentations of impressively rendered illustrations. The renderings invariably show sunlight slanting across broad plazas, trees in midsummer foliage perfectly framing the proposed building. Detailed models and grand plans drawn on large sheets of tracing paper may come to mind. These images do reflect the practice of architecture, but only a small part of it. Many of the services and products an architect provides are a lot less exciting than those sunlit plazas, but they are just as important.

Those other services include assisting you with such things as reroofing, recarpeting, and other maintenance projects. They encompass ADA evaluations, energy efficiency studies, interior design, furniture selection, signage consultation, landscape design, and assistance with grant applications. Sometimes the need for an architect may be questioned. A lot of your projects may not require the assistance of an architect, but some will benefit by having one to coordinate the work.

Let's study an example that illustrates the rationale for utilizing an architect. We'll take a reroofing project. First, let's establish the scene. You are asked to head the building and grounds committee of the Roosevelt Library District. The current roof on the library is over twenty years old. It's what is called a "built-up" roof, made up of layers of asphalt-impregnated fabric topped with gravel. It has given good service over the years with only a minimum of problems. Recently, however, more and more leaks have been appearing. Your building engineer, armed with large buckets of black, sticky roofing compound, has been making frequent trips up top to make repairs. In spite of her efforts, after every hard rain the staff reports more stained ceiling tiles, revealing the presence of new leaks. It's clearly time to do something about the situation.

Your library director wisely anticipated the problem in the long-term financial plan, so in this year's budget there is a $50,000 line item intended to cover the cost of a new roof. Most states require that public projects with an anticipated cost of over a set limit must be competitively bid. Your office manager has therefore had a notice printed in the local paper stating that bids for a new roof will be received at the library. It also specifies that the bids are to be delivered by 1:00 p.m. on April 1 and will be publicly opened immediately afterward. Prospective bidders can be seen on the roof, pacing off distances, inspecting flashings, and taking core samples to test for insulation that has been saturated with water. In the meantime, the increased foot traffic on the roof has caused even more leaks, and the staff is placing plastic sheets over the computers every night in case of rain.

April 1 arrives and by one o'clock four bids have arrived. The bidders are sitting in the conference room awaiting the opening. An additional bid is delivered at five minutes after the hour; the contractor explains that one of the bridges in town is closed and traffic is moving very slowly. Your office manager rejects the late bid, citing the one o'clock stipulation in the advertisement for bids. The roofer storms out, shouting that the advertisement never stated that late bids would be rejected and that you just might hear from his lawyer and that he's a taxpayer too, and that he helped raise money during the last referendum and that the other bidders aren't local anyway. The library director and several board members arrive (a little late thanks to traffic tie-ups), and soon everyone is ready to open the bids. The office manager opens the first envelope, which contains the ABC Roofing Company's bid, and reads the bid (see fig. 2-1).

The representative from ABC Roofing nods. "Built-up roofing, asphalt, felt, and gravel. Been around for a hundred years and it's still the best there is!" This doesn't sound too bad; it's the same kind of roof the library has had, your building engineer knows how to maintain it (you can see her in the back row nodding her agreement), and it costs less than the $50,000 set aside for the job.

The office manager opens and reads Ever-Dry's bid (see fig. 2-2). Ever-Dry is definitely more expensive than the first bid but they are including more, aren't they? The Ever-Dry man is in the audience. "EPDM is the state of the art in roofing membranes, a spin-off from the space program. It'll last a lot longer than those antique built-up systems." His tone reminds you of a recent convert to a fringe religious group, but he does have you wondering if the additional work he included might not be a good idea.

The bid from Joe's Roofing is read. It's the low bid so far (see fig. 2-3). Do you have to accept it even if it looks a little, well . . . unprofessional? Joe is in the audience. He's shifting back and forth in his seat, looking a little nervous. Maybe he's wondering if he missed something.

Finally, Best Roofing Company's bid is read (see fig. 2-4). This looks like a high-quality outfit, and at this price they had better be. Isn't the scope of work in this bid a lot like the second one, though? Why are the prices so different? This one is almost half again as much as Ever-Dry's price for what seems to be the same work. Something's not right here. The office manager clears her throat. "We will announce the selection of the roofing contractor at the board meeting next Tuesday night. Thank you for coming and thank you for your bids."

The building committee is scheduled to meet the day before the regular board meeting to evaluate the bids and arrive at their recommendation. As chair of the committee, you are expected to provide some leadership in the decision-making process, but where to start? The first bid was about what you expected and you felt good about it, at least until the second bid was opened. Then, the first in a series of uncomfortable questions began to crop up. You decide to write them down so you can address them one at a time. The list looks something like the following:

1. What is EPDM and, the Space Agency notwithstanding, is it any better than built-up roofing?

Figure 2-1

Figure 2-2

JOE'S ROOFING & BAIT

"Home of Bass-Oh-Matic™ Lures"

Bid for a new roof for the Rosevelt Library.

Bid includes:

Replacement of existing roof.
(New roof to match existing.)

Total cost: $22,750.00

Joe

Owner; Joe's Roofing & Bait

Outboard Engine Sales and Service

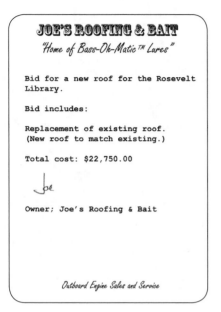

Figure 2-3

Best Roofing Inc.

"Serving Yourtown Since 1946"

Best Roofing Company is pleased to submit this bid for a new E.P.D.M. roof for the Roosevelt Memorial Library District. Bid includes:
Tear-off of existing roofing and insulation. Installation of new E.P.D.M. roofing membrane over new tapered insulation. Disposal of waste materials off-site. Repair of damaged flashing at North side of roof top mechanical unit. Work to be accomplished within 90 days of receipt of signed proposal.

Total installed cost: $57,000.00
All work covered under manufacturer's 20 year warrantee.

Signed;
H. Edward Forsythe III
President, Best Roofing Inc.

Fully insured and bonded
"Serving Yourtown Since 1946"
State Roofers License # 04-2990

Figure 2-4

2. What about the additional work Ever-Dry has included on their bid? Do we need new insulation or can the existing material be left on the roof?
3. What about the damaged flashing. Is it something that ABC would have included as a part of their work?
4. Is ABC's work guaranteed, and how much will it cost us to provide the dumpsters? Will a landfill accept the waste material?
5. Do we have to accept Joe's bid as legitimate? If so, are we legally obligated to take the lowest bid?
6. Some say they are insured. Some say they are bonded. Some say both, and some neither. How do we establish our minimum requirements?
7. Why are some of the bids for the same work so different? Do some of them misunderstand the scope of the work?
8. Joe's Roofing isn't a union shop. Do they have to be union in order to bid public work?
9. After we make the selection and the work begins, how do we know that we are getting what we paid for?
10. And what about that guy with the late bid, could he really sue us?

At this point you realize that this could go on for a long time with no real resolution. The most important question hasn't even been asked yet.

11. Which one do we recommend?

You might feel that you would be going out on a limb by making any choice based on what you currently know. There is no real way to compare the bids meaningfully. You were proud when they asked you to head the building committee, but now it doesn't seem like such an enviable position.

Role of the Architect

Even the seemingly straightforward task of getting a new roof can create a surprising number of complications. In our story you could substitute recarpeting, apparently minor ADA work, or even some interior remodeling for the reroofing project—and exactly the same problems might have arisen. If you can be held accountable for the money you are spending, you owe it to yourself to make sure all your decisions are based on informed, if not expert, opinion. This is where the concept of "expert insurance" applies.

Hiring a consultant may not only get you a better product, it can also insulate you from certain questions of liability. The role (and the goal) of the architect is to circumvent the kind of problems that you, as the head of the building committee, faced in the fictional reroofing project. A well-written advertisement for bids, backed with some drawings and a written specification, would have prevented most if not all of the difficulties. Except in cases where the law requires the use of a licensed architect or engineer (like constructing a new building or addition), the decision of when to use an architect may rest with the board. In cases like the reroofing project, the use of an architect may not be mandatory, but in light of the possible difficulties it may be advisable to hire one. For such projects it is always something of a judgment call. The best one can do is weigh the in-house expertise available against the potential risks and see where the balance lies. Let's summarize some of the advantages of retaining an architect:

- The architect will produce drawings and specifications that set minimum standards of quality for the project.

- The bids you receive will be more meaningful, reducing the chance that you will have to "compare apples and oranges."

- You will receive advice on the selection of materials and systems that are appropriate for your project.

- The architect will work to see that you receive the protection of manufacturer's warrantees and contractor's guarantees of which you otherwise might not be aware.

- If you wish, the architect can observe the work to confirm that it is being done correctly and in conformance with specifications; and you only approve payments to the contractor after the architect has verified the completion and adequacy of the work.

- Some products have federal or state standards that limit their use in certain locations, because of excessive flammability, for example, or other safety concerns. An architect's specifications will prohibit the use of such materials in the work.

- Using an architect will ensure that you have adequate records of work done. Old drawings and specifications are invaluable when you are considering an addition or remodeling.

> ### AMERICAN INSTITUTE OF ARCHITECTS
>
> The American Institute of Architects is a nationwide organization of architects, interns, and others involved with the practice of architecture. The organization is dedicated to advancing the profession of architecture, enhancing the professional growth of its members, and informing the public of the profession.
>
> Not every licensed architect has "AIA" after his or her name. Membership in the AIA is strictly voluntary, though many if not most licensed architects do belong to the organization.
>
> The AIA publishes a code of ethics for professional conduct that is intended to set basic standards of professional responsibilities: *The Architect's Handbook of Professional Practice* (Washington, D.C., 1993). Although the code is not legally binding, it is widely recognized by the profession. The legal responsibilities of the architect are determined by the licensing statutes of each state. The licensing statutes are more general than the AIA ethical standards and are typically intended to protect the health, safety, and welfare of the public.

These services are discussed in detail in chapter 3, where we review the parts of a typical building project. Although I have been speaking only of architects, the same reasoning applies to other professionals as well. New boilers require the services of a mechanical engineer; revisions to the building's electrical power system, an electrical engineer; sagging floors, a structural engineer; and so on. Some projects require numerous trades. One of the prime roles of the architect is to retain and coordinate the efforts of many different consultants. In addition to structural, mechanical, and electrical engineers, a project team may include civil engineers, acoustical engineers, plumbing engineers, landscape architects, building code consultants, and others. The architect usually retains the other consultants, and the board is thus spared the responsibility of having to investigate the qualifications and costs of what may be a large number of players. The responsibility of ensuring that these diverse groups perform as intended also rests with the architect. For these complicated projects, an architect offers what amounts to a "one-stop shopping" service. The architect provides the client with a single line of communication in place of what might otherwise be a confusing din of contractors, each demanding attention to help deal with their own problems.

Architect as Agent

During the course of a project, the architect acts on behalf of the client. This leads us to the special nature of the relationship between you and your architect. Your contract with the architect enables the architect to act as your agent. In the simplest sense, agency is the concept that two parties, the client and the architect, can have a relationship that enables an outside third party to accept the actions of the agent (the architect) as being binding on the principal (the client). The legal ramifications of agency can be complex, and it is vital that the board understand just what the architect is empowered to do in its name. When signing a contract with an architect or other professional, it is a good idea to meet with your legal counsel for advice on the terms of the proposed contract. Your counsel should give you an explanation in plain language of what actions the architect is empowered to take on your behalf. Standard architectural contracts are often modified to conform to the requirements of a particular project. Your counsel can advise you of any changes that should be made to suit your own situation.

Architect as Judge

There is one interesting twist in the standard contract. According to the "Standard Form of Agreement between Owner and Architect," as published by the AIA, there are situations in which the architect can be required to act as an impartial third party. (In AIA contract terminology, any client is referred to as the "owner.") This is particularly true when the architect must render an interpretation of the contract documents. According to the contract, when making such an interpretation the architect shall "endeavor to secure faithful performance by both Owner and Contractor, shall not show partiality to either, and shall not be liable for the results of interpretations or decisions so rendered in good faith" (AIA Document B141, Part 2.6.1.8).

Though the architect is working for the client, the architect cannot force the contractor to perform any service that is not reasonably inferable in the contract documents. This protects the contractor from arbitrary or capricious actions on the part of the client and is important in maintaining a productive and fair client/contractor relationship.

Chapter 3

Anatomy of a Project

An architectural project can be broken up into as many as nine distinct phases, each phase representing a different facet of the architect's services. It is important that you, as a potential client, have an understanding of the significance of each part, and of how it relates to the project as a whole. To get the maximum benefit from your architect, you should know in advance what should be happening at each phase. You should know what you can expect from the architect, and what your architect can expect from you.

AIA Contracts and Architectural Services

Those of you who have worked with an architect in the past may be surprised to learn that the AIA made some significant changes in its standard Owner/Architect contract, one of these changes involving project phases. Formerly, phases (schematic design, construction documents, bidding, etc.) were defined by the AIA contract and used as a basis for determining the timing of payments to the architect. These definitions have been removed from the new standard contract. And though they are no longer in the AIA contract, most architects still define their work in terms of these phases. The chapters of this book are organized in this manner—by phase.

In the remainder of this book, I discuss services the architect might provide as a part of each phase of the project. Previous versions of the standard AIA Owner/Architect contract defined services that were traditionally included as part of a contract with an architect as "basic services." Other services that were less commonly included in a standard AIA contract were called "additional services." This approach changed with the release of the 1997 version of the standard Owner/Architect contract. The distinction between "basic" and "additional" services has changed. Now services that are applicable to a project are identified and assembled into an inclusive list of exactly what services the architect will be required to perform under the contract. To aid you in drawing up the contract, the AIA offers a "shopping list" of the most common tasks architects perform. With this arrangement, you begin your contract negotiations by sitting down with your architect and identifying those services that you both agree are required. In this book, I use the term "basic services" to describe those services that are part of nearly every architectural contract. I also describe less common services (formally "additional services") to help illustrate other services your architect can provide should they apply to your situation.

Milestones and Millstones

The end of each phase represents an identifiable milestone in the course of a project. Meetings should be scheduled with the architect at these points to ensure that the entire board is following the course of the project. These meetings also allow you to verify that the architect is producing the product for which you are paying. It is advisable that the board sign off on the project at the end of each phase, for several reasons. A formal sign-off on the project to date can help push members of the board to spend the time to really understand what has been done and the direction in which the project is going. Another reason is to protect the architect. If the board should change its mind about some aspect of the project after signing off on the work, the architect could justifiably ask for additional fees for redesign. The formal sign-off also helps reduce the chance of misunderstandings regarding the scope of the work and potential requests for additional fees.

Keeping up with a complex project can be time consuming, but it is mandatory for those who carry the public trust and spend the public's money. Sticking with it and doing a thorough job at each milestone is the best way to keep current with your project. Because you will often be called on to make decisions regarding the work, you should have a thorough understanding of the state of your project at all times. Spending the time as it is required keeps you informed of the progress and prevents those milestones from becoming millstones.

Chapter 4

Programming

T. S. Eliot might well have been speaking of the information age. We are over-whelmed with information. Some of it is useful to us; the larger part of it, however, blends into a sort of data-laden noise that we have grown adept at tuning out. In the simplest sense, *architectural programming* is the process of sifting the pertinent data from the noise: collecting data, sorting out that which is relevant to the current project, and using it as a basis for design. But this is a rather dry definition for what can be a satisfying and enjoyable experience.

Programming is also the most interactive phase of an architectural project. For the future users of the building, it is a time of both self-expression and self-examination, as they look at themselves and try to identify their needs, desires, and dreams. To ensure that the right information is collected in an efficient way, the programmer and client should together establish a formalized procedure for collecting data.

A building program can be produced by a library building consultant, a professional programmer, or an architect. For most types of projects, architects tend to do their own programming. In the case of libraries, however, the programming is sometimes done by a library building consultant. This depends partly on the requirements of your state library. In some states the participation of a library building consultant is required to qualify the project for public grant money. When a library building consultant is used, the architect uses the consultant's report as a starting point and then expands it in producing the architectural program. For the sake of simplicity, in this chapter I refer to the architect as the programmer. Whether it is done by an architect, a professional programmer, or a library building consultant, programming is the essential first step in the design process.

What Is a Building Program?

A completed building program is usually in the form of a written document. Sometimes it is primarily text; sometimes it has accompanying diagrams. The program sets out the special requirements for the building. These requirements are established through research and interviews with people who will use the building. The following are some of the most important categories of information your building program should address:

GENERAL STATEMENT OF GOALS. The goals for the building should be stated. This is especially important because it verifies that the architect, users, and board of directors all have the same expectations for what the building should be and how the building should work. If you have a long-term plan, the programmer should be aware of the plan and incorporate it into the programming process.

SPATIAL REQUIREMENTS. The building program should define each significant room in the planned structure as well as exterior spaces that are important in the function of the building. The estimated area for each space should be given.

ADJACENCIES AND ROOM RELATIONSHIPS. Adjacency requirements describe how each space must relate to the other spaces around it. There are several ways rooms

Well begun is half done.
—Aristotle

Where is the wisdom that we have lost in knowledge? Where is the knowledge that we have lost in information?
—T. S. Eliot

can relate to each other. Some situations may require good visual communication from one room to another. Other times, the rooms may need to be visually or acoustically isolated. One room might require easy access to one of its neighbors but complete separation from another. Sometimes rooms must be placed in close proximity; sometimes they must be separated by as much distance as possible. Adjacency requirements can be expressed in written form, with matrices, or in graphics such as bubble diagrams.

An adjacency matrix (figure 4-1) is usually generated before a bubble diagram. In it, the name of each significant room or space in the proposed building is listed on each row and each column of a grid. The names for each of the rooms thus cross somewhere on the matrix. At this intersection, a symbol indicates the nature of the relationship between the two rooms. After the adjacency matrix is complete, the architect can begin to prepare a bubble diagram (figure 4-2). Although it is not a floor plan, a bubble diagram goes one step beyond an adjacency matrix by indicating something about the path one must take to get to a particular space. As an example, an adjacency matrix might indicate that the lobby and the entry vestibule are related and need to be placed in close proximity. It would take a bubble diagram, however, to indicate that a person can get to the lobby only by going through the vestibule.

ROOM AMENITIES. The program should give detailed information about other features requested by the client, including such things as number and sizes of windows, interior finishes, casework, closets, and lighting requirements.

MECHANICAL, ELECTRICAL, AND PLUMBING. Special requirements for mechanical, electrical, and plumbing systems should be given. Special electrical and cooling provisions for a computer room are an example, as is a filtered air system for a hospital operating room. A typical library staff room may have several items that fit in this category, including a sink, water supply and drain connections for a refrigerator icemaker, 220-volt electrical supply for an electric oven, telephone jack, and public address system speaker. Many items that come under this classification are things that are either out of sight or that one tends to take for granted. Your architect can help you to identify your requirements.

FURNISHINGS. Often building programs include information regarding furnishings. Even if they are not responsible for selecting the furnishings, architects usually collect information about anticipated furnishings as an aid in determining the required dimensions for each space. The information tabulated in the program can be a valuable resource for the user in establishing the amount of furniture that must be purchased.

One special "furnishing" deserves mention: art. A commitment could be made at this time to include original art as a part of your building. Original artwork can take many forms in a building project. Paintings, murals, or sculpture in the lobby come to mind immediately, but it can take other, less orthodox forms. Some successful bas relief forms have been sculpted into face brick. Decorative tilework, sometimes with handmade tiles, can add interest to a wall or floor. An impressive piece of custom woodwork for a circulation desk could be commissioned. If local artists and artisans can be utilized, including them in the project can be a good way to stimulate public interest and support for your project.

SITE DEVELOPMENT. The building program should address the relationship between the building and the site. As a practical matter, providing adequate parking should always be considered—although there is an interesting twist to this argument when we discuss sustainable design (see chapter 13). Access to and from

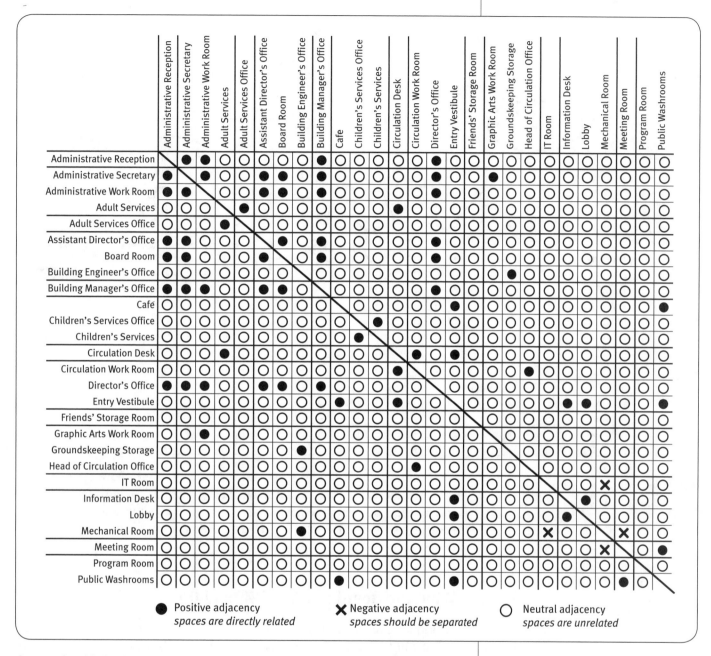

Figure 4-1
Sample adjacency matrix

the site should also be considered. There may be external restrictions that control where access points can be located. As an example, it is often difficult to gain permission from municipal authorities to provide new curb cuts onto busy streets. Local zoning restrictions also have to be taken into account, since they often limit the maximum amount of area a building can occupy on a site and mandate set-back distances from the property lines and permissible building heights. Though site design really begins later in the process with the schematic design, the client should express any desires or preconceptions relating to site development during the programming phase. Be sure to remember to include landscape design in your programming. All too often, landscape development is added as an afterthought or omitted entirely. When added as an afterthought, it is often the first thing cut if there is a budget crunch later on. We take a closer look at the importance of landscaping when we discuss site analysis in chapter 5.

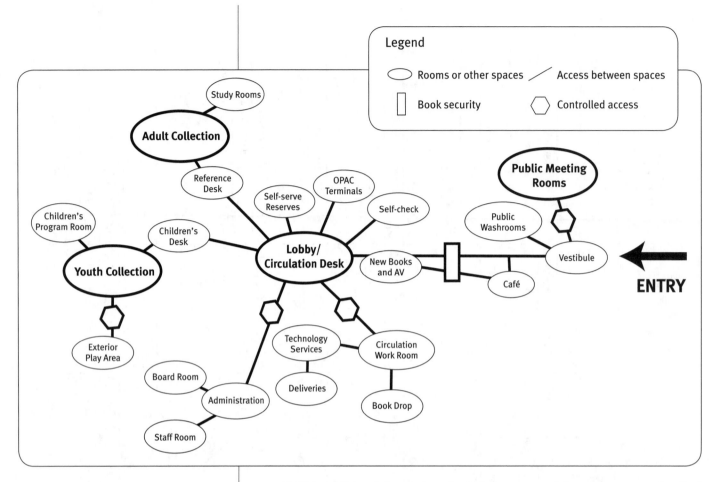

Legend

⬭ Rooms or other spaces ╱ Access between spaces

▯ Book security ⬡ Controlled access

Figure 4-2
Sample bubble diagram

OTHER. Additional items that don't fit into any of the above categories find their way into the "other" classification. Nearly anything could be included here: special safety or security requirements, information about unusual floor loadings (e.g., high structural loads from compact shelving), or unusual acoustical requirements.

What the Board and Staff Should Do

Before programming can begin, there are several things the board and staff should do:

IDENTIFY PROJECT GOALS. The board should discuss the intended scope of the program statement with the programmer/architect before programming begins. Doing so helps ensure that all the data you think are important are going to be collected; it also aids you in planning the amount of time library staff must devote to the process.

In chapter 3 we spoke of "a house divided" and discussed the importance of having the support of the entire board and staff. Assuming that everyone is in favor of the project, this is the time to verify that there is agreement on the project goals. Examine your reasons for undertaking the project; these should be agreed on in advance and will determine the conceptual "blueprint" for the project. Put your project goals in writing and refer to them from time to time to verify that the project is proceeding according to your plans.

IDENTIFY WHAT YOU HAVE. While identifying the project goals, spend some time identifying good and bad aspects of your current facilities. Identify things that work well for you and things that don't. Discuss the reasons for the shortcomings and successes and commit them to writing. These will be valuable clues for the programmer and architect that help them tailor the programming to your project.

BRAINSTORM. Get your staff together for some brainstorming sessions to identify their concerns and discuss their ideas. Include staff members that might not be scheduled for interviews with the programmer to ensure that they have a chance to contribute their input. Distribute the project goals to staff members. This gives them an overview of what programming is about and facilitates your brainstorming sessions.

PUT TOGETHER YOUR PROJECT TEAM. During the programming process, the architect interviews board and staff members to identify your needs. To control the process, it is important to develop a list of responsibilities and assign them to members of your in-house team. It is critical that all the data generated in-house be reviewed before an architect is eventually given the authority to act on this information. Questions that must be answered include the following:

- Who will talk to the programmer? The board and library director will probably be interviewed, but there are many others who should have input. Department heads should be on the list. Have them submit names of other staffers who they feel will contribute to the process. Staff members responsible for particular aspects of the library (like the computer system) should be included. The building engineer and others responsible for maintenance issues should also be interviewed.

- What is the chain of command? Each person's contributions should be reviewed by the immediate superior to ensure conformity to the overall goals of the project. This process should extend up to and including the board members, with their ideas being reviewed by the board as a whole.

- Who will organize the effort? Assign an individual at the library the task of coordinating the interviews. Interviews and data collection can be time consuming. They must be scheduled, and the staff involved must be allotted time for their participation. Determine a master schedule with your programmer. Set a completion date and allot the time required to keep to your schedule.

Information-Gathering Tools

The prime information-gathering tool of the programmer is the interview. In addition to the interview, the programmer may develop questionnaires and distribute them for the staff to complete. These questionnaires may address physical requirements for the building as well as staff and patron activities that take place within the library. The data from the questionnaires and interviews will be evaluated, and often the information is later summarized by the architect.

When the programmer has completed the information-gathering portion of the programming phase, the next step is to assemble the information into a preliminary program document that summarizes the data; see appendix E for a sample program summary sheet. This first compilation of the program represents the client's wish list. If the programmer is someone other than the architect, this document should be shared with the architect to give the first indications of the size of the building and likely scope of the furniture and equipment packages. This information can be used to arrive at a first rough estimate of the project cost.

There is often a moment of truth the first time your dream is measured against your budget. There might not be a defined budget at this point, in which case the cost figures generated could be turned over to your financial consultant to determine the feasibility of the project. After that, the feasibility is measured against available or anticipated resources, including the perceived chances of passing a referendum. Sometimes the cost of the proposed building exceeds the potential financial resources.

Now the architect and client have to sit down to make some hard decisions regarding the preliminary program. Square footages may have to be trimmed, and some of the "bells and whistles" may have to be cut out entirely. The staff can be expected to do some internal lobbying for personal favorites. The final decisions as to what constitutes "bells and whistles" may have to be made by the library director and board. And sometimes the cuts must go beyond the frills and begin to erode important program elements. Your architect can help show you the costs associated with different parts of the project and assist you in your decision making.

It is important to bring the project within the anticipated budget before completing the program phase. Indeed, it is wise to establish a contingency of 5–15 percent of the projected cost to make up for unanticipated cost overruns later. It can be tempting to proceed with the project when it is slightly over the proposed budget in the optimistic belief that the costs can be brought down by tightening up the design later. Unfortunately, it usually goes the other way. Inevitably, things are forgotten or otherwise unaccounted for during programming, and they tend to get added to the building later. Taken singly they seem insignificant, but en masse they can put your project over budget.

A Cautionary Note

The process of deleting items from your building program can be difficult. The building program produced thus far still represents the wish list of the people interviewed. It is a snapshot view of wishes and perceived needs of the library's users and staff at a particular point in time. It is thus imperative that flexibility be designed into the program to account for future needs.

One must remember that, in time, needs will change. It also must be noted that the current staff (including the board and library director) will change with the passage of time. Sometimes a building program can be unduly influenced by one or two people with strong personalities and set ideas. Remember that the building program you are developing now will have an impact on future generations of library staff, library directors, board members, and, most important, the public. In that light, all programming decisions should be measured against the perceived benefits for future users and administrators of the institution.

It is not uncommon to find yourself having to navigate some difficult political waters at this time. Helping to bring resolution to difficult questions of priorities is one of the skills of a good architect. Let your architect guide the process and take the heat if need be. After all, leadership is one of the qualities for which you are paying.

The Cost Estimate

As the program begins to take shape, the architect can start supplying information about anticipated costs. It is an easy matter to take the total square footage from the preliminary building program, multiply by an assumed cost per square foot, and come up with a rough estimate of the building cost. The multiplication is simple; selecting the appropriate cost per square foot is not.

Many factors influence the estimated cost per square foot. The size of the project, the geographic locale, the anticipated level of difficulty to construct the project, and the relative expense of the interior finishes are a few of the factors that must be taken into account. These factors are always used along with general cost data from other local projects that are similar to your own.

You can find published sample costs per square foot for different types of construction, but you must use such information with care. The effects of inflation can cause published numbers to be misleading in these matters. One standard source printed in 1977 states that a library of "superb" quality can be built for $70 per square foot. Depending on the circumstances, in 2007 that number might be more than $250 per square foot. I caution the reader to take all published cost numbers with a grain of salt.

If you multiply a reasonable cost per square foot by the total area itemized in your building program, you get a number which, at first glance, seems to indicate the construction cost for your project. However, the analysis so far is lacking an important factor: building efficiency.

Building Efficiency

The cost calculation mentioned above is based on the total of the program areas of the building; the square footage for each office, lobby, reading room, and so on is added up to produce a total program area. The term "program area" is significant. The building will be significantly larger than the program area. Just how much larger depends on the building efficiency.

Building efficiency is defined as the net square footage (the areas described in the building program) divided by the gross area of the building. The gross area of the building includes not only the total of the areas from your building program but the area occupied by mechanical spaces, corridors, walls, storage areas, toilets, stairways, elevators, shafts, ducts, and anything else not addressed in the program document. When including these other areas, your 40,000-square-foot library (net) may suddenly become a 66,000-square-foot building (gross), and your budget may suddenly look a lot more restrictive than it did a moment ago.

In this example, the building efficiency would be expressed by the following:

Building Efficiency = Net Area divided by Gross Area
Building Efficiency = 40,000 sq ft / 66,000 sq ft = 0.61, or 61 percent

Now you've got a number, 61 percent, but what does it mean? An opulent structure with wide hallways, expansive lobbies, and sweeping stairways has a relatively low efficiency ratio because of the percentage of the area taken up by those amenities. A warehouse with a large, open area and few hallways or other distractions has a high efficiency. In a crude sense, the efficiency of your building is a reflection of the efficiency of your use of the public's money. The analogy is too limited to be of much use, because few people would propose a warehouse for their public library, regardless of the efficiency of the building. On the other hand, the public might not support a grandiose structure for a small town library even if the municipal coffers would allow it. Building efficiencies typically range from 90 to 50 percent, depending on the building type. Describing efficiencies with appropriate adjectives is one of the best ways to visualize what the numbers mean. For a library, the following might be a rough guide:

BUILDING EFFICIENCY	DESCRIPTION
50 percent	Opulent, grand
60 percent	Monumental public building
65 percent	Comfortable
75 percent	Economical
80 percent	Spartan
85 percent or higher	Probably impossible to attain for a public library

The building efficiency has a direct bearing on the public's perception of your library. The perception is equally colored by the selection of the interior finish materials. An expansive space with an opulent efficiency but cheap materials might strike them as stark rather than grand. A small, efficient building finished with interesting, high-quality materials might come off as comfortable and rich in detail.

Discuss the building efficiency with your architect. You need address the issue only in the most general of terms. As long as the board of directors understands the balance between building efficiency, economy, and public perception, they can arrive at informed decisions regarding their building. When looking at an architect's space analysis of your project, you should understand the architect's assumed efficiency figure—and in that way verify that you and the architect have similar ideas about what kind of building you are developing.

Library programmers often assume a particular building efficiency in their program to get an approximation of the eventual size of the building. This is a handy first intimation of building size, but it needs to be understood as a very rough first estimate. Until the actual design of the library is begun, many factors—currently unknown to the programmer—can effect building efficiency. A good example is a small building site. A tight building site may cause a relatively small library that would usually be built on a single level to become a two-story building. The addition of at least two stairways, an elevator, and an elevator equipment room might add 500–700 square feet to the size of the library as estimated by the library programmer. This area represents *unassignable* square footage—that is, area that cannot be assigned to a particular library function but is required to satisfy other criteria. This increases the gross area but not the net area of the building and results in a lower building efficiency. If your programmer has not included a factor for building efficiency in the library program, I recommend that the programmer's estimate of the library size be increased by at least 20 percent until the building efficiency is tested during the design phase.

The Final Product

After you have completed the difficult process of reducing your square footage to fall within your budget and agreed on a target building efficiency, your architect can produce the final program document. This combination of written and graphic material provides the foundation on which the rest of the architectural project is built. The document includes many of the items that have been discussed here as well as additional information that is applicable to your project. At this point you and your architect have the information to describe what will go into the building or addition and a good idea of its potential cost. See chapter 14 for a detailed discussion about building costs.

Sign-Off

You should now schedule a board meeting so the board of trustees as well as management staff can sign off on the project to date. All people involved should be given a copy of the document a week or so in advance to allow everyone to have a chance to review the material thoroughly. Ideally, major changes suggested in previous reviews have been incorporated into the document. If any other changes seem required, make a written list of them, attach them to a copy of the program, and give an additional copy of the changes to the architect. Have the board members and management staff sign the master program document to indicate their acceptance of it. This master copy of the program with attached changes should be retained for reference. Any changes to the program after acceptance could provide a legitimate basis for the architect to bill you for the additional time involved in rewriting parts of the program.

Chapter 5

Site Analysis

I'll never forget a story that was related to me by an acquaintance. He was the structural engineer for a new office building in Chicago. The building site had been selected and purchased by the owner. The location was perfect, and tenants were already lining up to sign leases. Small structures on the site had been razed, and several borings had been taken to test the strength of the underlying soil and rock. All appeared well. Construction schedules were established, manpower mobilized, and building permits obtained. The schedule was tight, but with good weather the building could be finished on time. A construction fence was erected around the construction site. The fence was solid wood with the obligatory peepholes cut into it so children and other interested passersby could keep track of the work. Early one weekend morning, large, costly excavating equipment was brought in. Everything was ready.

Just after dawn on Monday morning, the excavators arrived. Equipment was checked, and the air filled with blue diesel smoke as cold engines were started. The time clocks started ticking as the hourly rates for the large machinery kicked in, and across town the first dump trucks were on their way to pick up the excavated material. The work began well, and a steady stream of trucks rumbled back and forth past glass-fronted office buildings.

He got the phone call at around ten that morning. Arriving at the construction site, he saw a group of workers standing around the excavation, looking in the hole. The diesel engines had been shut down, and there was a line of dump trucks waiting to be filled. Nothing was moving except the clock. It's not unusual to find pieces of old foundations while excavating in an urban setting. This was, however, much more than a piece. Partially exposed at the bottom of the hole was a mass of concrete. There, neatly sandwiched between the locations of their soil borings, was a foundation of a turn-of-the-century railroad roundhouse. The foundation was many feet thick and liberally reinforced with what appeared to be railroad rails.

Blasting is discouraged in most downtown areas, so the only thing to do was jackhammer it into small pieces and truck it away, a time-consuming and expensive proposition. The construction schedule was shot, and the cost of the additional work would have to be borne by the owner. The excavators drove away, the dump trucks rumbled off, even the sidewalk superintendents at the peepholes went home. The engineer was left with the unenviable task of having to call the owner with the news. The frustrated building owner in the story might also have thought, "This is the place!" when he first saw the site. It was just that there was a lot more to the place than was apparent. There's no guarantee that a site analysis will protect you from surprises like this one, but it will at least help tip the scales in your favor.

In chapter 4, we touched on the importance of the relationship between a building and its site. For a building project, site analysis is one of the first steps in the design process. Like programming, much of site analysis involves the collection and interpretation of data. Some information is readily accessible and some requires detective work, intuition, and the assistance of specialized consultants.

A site analysis includes much more than a search for forgotten foundations. In a moment, I discuss the scope of a complete site analysis and what the board should be doing during this phase; but first, let's talk about the role of another design professional, the landscape architect.

The Landscape Architect

For the sake of simplicity, I'm using the word "architect" to denote the person providing your site analysis. Many times the analysis is provided by an architect, but often much of the work is done by a landscape architect. Like architects, landscape architects are trained in design, but their focus is on site development and plant materials. Although architects often produce site designs, the special skills and expertise of the landscape architect can make this individual especially suited for inclusion in the site analysis. If you are not contemplating a building project but are just looking for ways to spruce up the look of your building, consider retaining a landscape architect to suggest some ways to make better use of your site. First impressions do count, and the first impression of a building is often a reaction to the landscaping rather than to the structure itself.

What the Board Should Do

Even a building addition requires a site analysis, but for the moment let's assume that you are purchasing a new site for your project. You've probably looked around town for appropriate sites and maybe even set a realtor on the scent. Imagine that two potential sites seem to stand out from the others, and now it only remains to decide between those two.

In a case like this, it may be advisable to have your architect do a partial analysis for each site and apply a numerical ranking to the different aspects studied. With this method, the choice between the sites might be easier if there is a clear winner when the scores are added up. If there is no clear winner, you at least have a lot more information to factor into your decision making. You can discuss the thoroughness of each partial site analysis with your architect and decide on the minimum number of aspects that might be investigated in order to provide enough data to allow you to make an informed decision. In this case, you reserve the complete site analysis for the selected site and thus reduce your expenses for professional services.

While narrowing down the number of sites, the board should discuss the project and how they imagine the building would relate to each candidate site. Several factors enter into the selection of a building site: emotional reactions to different parts of town, political factors, historical significance, cost of the site, and ease of access, to name a few. These subjects alone can provide the basis for a lot of discussion, and other aspects will no doubt surface as well.

What You Should Provide

An architect usually begins a thorough site analysis only after the client has provided certain preliminary information. For example, the client customarily pays for and obtains soil borings and a survey of the property. The architect needs this information as early as possible to do a site analysis. If the library hasn't yet purchased the property, the current owner may be able to provide a survey and may even be persuaded to pay for the cost of the soil borings. The locations and number of the soil borings are usually suggested by the architect on the basis of the potential placement of the building and other site improvements. Ask your architect if there are any other pieces of information needed up front. An environmental assessment of the site may also be required; if so, your architect and local building authorities can put you in contact with an appropriate consultant. (In this context, "environmental assessment" generally means a search for buried tanks, polluted soil, and the like; more on this below.)

If you are building an addition to your existing facility or own the property on which you propose to build, this is the time to order a survey of your building or property. Your architect can assist you in retaining a surveyor if you do not already have one. If you already have an up-to-date survey, a new one may not be required; again, your architect can help you determine if any existing surveys are suitable.

What the Architect Should Do

A complete site analysis covers aspects ranging from the aesthetic to the technical. Often the architect will be assembling a team of other professionals from various fields, including landscape architects, civil engineers, land planners, soils engineers, and environmental engineers. The graphic portion of a site analysis is shown in figure 5-1.

Most architects include site analysis as part of the overall design process, but find out if yours does. If your situation requires the architect to analyze several sites, you will probably have to pay for additional professional services. When negotiating a contract with the architect, make sure everyone has the same understanding of which services are going to be provided as a part of the basic package and which ones will incur additional fees.

The first step in the site analysis is a careful examination of the building program. The program can determine, to a large extent, how a site will be utilized. The architect must then determine if the building program and site are compatible. Each must be evaluated with respect to the other. If preliminary work establishes that the program and site are compatible, the process of site analysis and design can begin.

The first thing the architect may do is verify that the building and other planned improvements will fit on the site. Many other site deficiencies can be remedied given enough money, but if the space is too small, the rest of the site analysis is rendered a moot point. It is not usually a problem to get the building itself on the site; the problem often lies in accommodating the parking lot. The exact number of parking spaces required is often set by local zoning ordinances. The percentage of a modern site covered by parking space can be shocking. For many projects, parking lots occupy over twice the area covered by the building. This situation seems unlikely to change as long as the family car remains the primary mode of transportation; unless that fact is altered, we will continue (in the words of Joni Mitchell) to "pave paradise and put up a parking lot."

In addition to parking lots, another factor that can reduce the amount of buildable area on your potential site is storm water detention. Most parts of the country require that building sites over a certain minimum size provide some sort of storm water detention. Essentially, storm water detention involves slowing down the rate at which rain that falls on your site runs off either onto adjacent properties or into storm sewers. When impermeable surfaces (e.g., rooftops, parking lots) are placed on a previously virgin site, water runs off the site much more rapidly than before

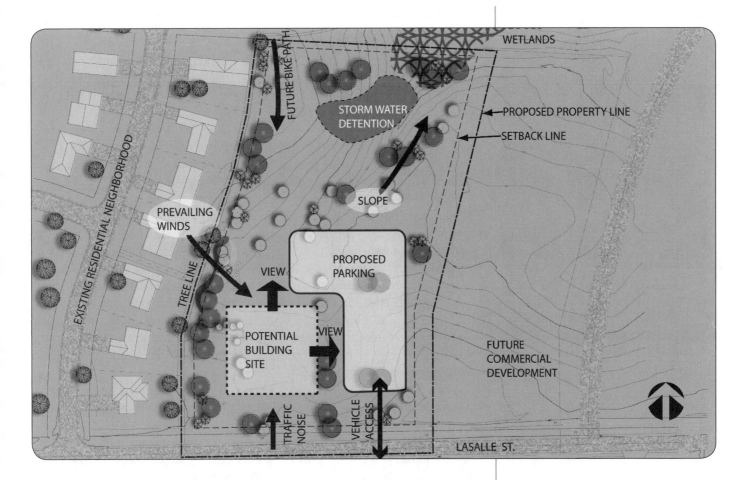

Figure 5-1

Sample site analysis

and contributes to flooding problems downstream. In this case, "downstream" can be anything from the next-door neighbor to the lower end of town to the mouth of the Mississippi.

The most common type of storm water detention is a grassy detention basin. Rainwater from your site is directed into this basin. Somewhere in the detention area, a pipe drains the collected water to the edge of the site or directly to a storm sewer. This pipe is intentionally undersized to slow the exit speed of the water to no more than it would have been had nothing been built on the site. After a significant rain, a detention area may have water in it for some time.

Our concern here is that, like the parking lot, this detention area takes up space. Between storm water detention and parking lots, many sites have a lot less buildable area than first seems to be the case. When space is tight, some of the detention can take place on top of the parking lot or under the lot in buried pipes. As you might imagine, the under-lot solution can be a lot more expensive than providing a grass basin to collect the storm water.

Site Analysis Checklist

The following is a checklist of some items that should be considered in a site analysis. Discuss the list with your architect to verify the depth of the analysis to be provided. If something you think is important is left out, ask that it be included. If you are buying a building site and haven't retained an architect yet, this list may be used as an initial guide to aid you with your site selection.

☑ *Existing conditions*

SIZE. As mentioned above, the size of the site is one of the most basic considerations. The true buildable area may be smaller than is apparent. In addition to parking lots and storm water detention areas, many of the factors listed below affect the buildable area of the site.

FLOODPLAINS. If some of the building site is in a floodplain, that portion is usually unusable for construction. Parking lots may sometimes be constructed on a floodplain. The architect researches the site to determine the existence and extent of floodplains and the local regulations regarding building on them.

WETLANDS. If your site has any designated wetlands on it, you are usually prohibited from building on those areas. In certain circumstances, a building can be put in a wetlands area if another area is "transformed" into a wetland. This transformation from regular land to wetland is somewhat controversial and may eventually be disallowed by the federal government. A word of warning: You cannot always determine what is and what is not a wetlands area by a casual inspection of the site. Standing water is only one clue that the site may contain wetlands. The types of plant growing on the site as well as soil types are also relevant. To the layperson it may in fact seem somewhat arbitrary whether a site is designated a wetland. Be that as it may, the site must be evaluated for wetlands before any building plans are considered.

ENDANGERED SPECIES. The potential effect of the project on endangered species is also evaluated. This evaluation as well as the wetlands study is usually performed by an environmental engineer whose work is coordinated by the architect.

AVAILABILITY OF UTILITIES. For most urban sites, utilities are available for your use. In rural and suburban settings, however, the type and capacity of the utilities around your site can impose serious limitations on your project. The team put together by your architect makes a thorough investigation of these utilities and incorporates the data they collect into their site analysis.

The utilities they study include electrical supplies, natural gas, water, telephone, data, sanitary sewer, and storm sewer. The sewer systems are investigated by the architect's civil engineer. Natural gas and electrical services are researched by the architect's mechanical and electrical engineers, respectively. Site analysis, like much of architecture, is a group effort. Your architect is responsible for ensuring that all the varied players are working in concert and in accordance with the building program.

UTILITY EASEMENTS. Your seemingly wide-open site may have a natural gas pipeline, water main, fiber-optic cables, or buried electrical lines running through it or along one of the property lines. An easement of a defined width prohibits any construction over or near the utility. These utilities may already exist, or there may be easements set in place for future utility work. The site survey should identify such easements.

OWNERSHIP. Before purchasing property, you must confirm that all the property you plan to buy is actually owned by the seller. This sounds like common sense, but there are instances where the true ownership of a piece of property was a surprise to everyone involved. A title search identifies any parts of the property that have been subdivided and sold off sometime in the past. Even when everyone involved has the best of intentions, a forgotten property transaction can come to light that shows that the prospective seller does not actually own everything that is for sale. I have encountered this several times when the sellers were, of all things, churches. In those cases, parts of the property had been sold off by some long-dissolved building committee and the records of the transactions subsequently misplaced. It wasn't until a title search was performed that the buyers and sellers learned that there was now a third property owner in the equation.

SUBSURFACE INVESTIGATIONS. Soil borings provide information on the capacity of the soil to support a building. They also identify the level of the water table, which may have a significant effect on the cost of constructing a basement.

TOPOGRAPHY. The topography of the site is analyzed to determine its impact on the proposed development. A hilly site can be more aesthetically pleasing than a flat one, but the costs of earthmoving for the building and parking lots go up. The difficulty of making the site accessible to the handicapped is also increased.

☑ *History of the site*

FORMER USES. Research into the former uses of a site is invaluable. There are a multitude of items (including foundations from railroad roundhouses) that might lie just below the surface. Subsurface surprises are almost never welcome ones, bits of old foundations and landfills being more commonly found than buried treasure. The architect may spend time studying old surveys, fire insurance maps, atlases, and city directories, attempting to identify what was there. For rural sites there is usually little information to go on, and few problems are typically encountered. For urban sites the research may be in depth and the risks higher.

BURIED TANKS AND HAZARDOUS MATERIALS. Finding that there was formerly a gas station or oil company on your site is often an indication of troubles ahead. Federal environmental legislation mandates that you remove buried tanks and clean up chemical contamination. There are also other, less obvious hazards like solvents and heavy metal contamination from old factories. There was a good example of this in my hometown of Elgin, Illinois. A project on the former site of the Elgin National Watch Company suffered long delays because it was discovered that watch dials and radium had been dumped on portions of the site when the factory was in operation. Construction was halted until the material could be removed and taken to special hazardous waste landfills, not an inexpensive undertaking.

LANDFILLS. It is amazing how often old landfills turn up. Most of them were not the municipal operations that are now the norm. Landfilling was, until recently, the accepted way to both get rid of your garbage and raise the grade of part of your property to make it more usable. Foundations cannot be placed on fill material, so the material must be removed before a building can go up. Soil borings identify old landfills.

ARCHEOLOGICAL CONSIDERATIONS. In many states an archeological inventory of the site is mandatory. Finding that there is a Native American burial ground or the remains of a frontier settlement on your property is intellectually stimulating, but it often means long delays before construction can begin while the artifacts are inventoried and studied or removed. Contractors know this, and there are many stories of excavation work speeding up dramatically in an effort to remove old bones or pottery shards before anyone else spots them. The archeological inventory is often provided by the state, and thus it must often be scheduled well in advance of construction.

A HIGH-TECH SOLUTION

Until recently, test excavations and soil borings were the only reliable ways to probe the subsurface mysteries of a site. Both methods involve heavy equipment and can be disruptive to the site. There are now several noninvasive tools that can speed up the process and are less expensive than soil borings. One is essentially a large magnetic anomaly detector—a large version of the metal detectors beachcombers use for searching for loose change and lost rings. This tool, which can be mounted on a large pole and carried around the site by a technician, is useful for finding buried tanks and other metallic objects. Another new tool is a mobile ground-penetrating radar unit mounted on a vehicle or hand-pushed cart. Ground-penetrating radar can identify buried items and determine the depth of the local bedrock. With these systems, large sites can be studied quickly to lessen the chance of subsurface surprises. Neither of these tools, however, can determine the strength of the soil and its capacity to carry foundations; soil borings are still required for that purpose.

☑ *Municipal restrictions*

ALLOWABLE USES. Local zoning ordinances usually define the allowable uses of a site. One begins by finding the zoning classification for the site. Zoning classifications usually look something like "B-1" (most likely a business zoning) or "R-2" (probably zoning for two-family residential units). Within each zoning classification there is usually a list of permitted uses. I have never seen anything like an "L-1" zoning classification to indicate a part of town set aside exclusively for libraries; libraries are usually listed as a permitted use under one of the other zoning classifications.

If your community's zoning ordinances state that libraries are a permitted use under B-1 zoning, and the site you want to purchase has a different classification, you may need to apply for a zoning variance or a zoning change in order to build your library there. This is not an unusual procedure, but it can take several months for your case to work its way through the various government bodies that must approve your request. There is also no guarantee of success. *If a zoning variance is required for you to use the property for your library, consider making the purchase of the property contingent on a successful outcome to your rezoning request.*

SETBACKS. Local zoning restrictions often stipulate how far a building must be set back from the property lines. These setbacks can prohibit construction on a significant percentage of the site. Setbacks tend to be the greatest from busy roads or residential areas. The architect's site analysis should identify required setbacks.

ALLOWABLE BUILDING AREA. Zoning restrictions often stipulate the maximum percentage of a site that can be covered by a building. On a tight site, it is possible that your proposed design would exceed the maximum building area permitted. Appealing for a zoning variance is your recourse if you run afoul of these regulations.

HISTORIC DISTRICTS. If your site is in a designated historic district, there may be regulations that limit your building design to particular architectural styles, building materials, or maximum heights. A study of any applicable historic district restrictions as well as the other municipal restrictions should be a part of the architect's zoning analysis.

☑ *Site accessibility and circulation*

ACCESS TO THE SITE. Easy site access is an integral part of serving the public. Access should be available to both vehicles and pedestrians. Traffic flow to your site is out of your control, but you can control circulation within your site. In chapter 4, I mentioned the potential problem of obtaining curb cuts onto busy thoroughfares. There are other considerations that must be negotiated with state and local authorities. If your library is on a heavily traveled street, you may wish to investigate the possibility of getting turning lanes at your entry points, or a traffic light. The architect can coordinate these negotiations for you.

Because you could be dealing with city, township, county, or state agencies, there can be a long lead time in obtaining curb cuts, turning lanes, or traffic lights. This assumes, of course, that the authorities have agreed to your requests. Sometimes they won't. If the site you want to purchase absolutely requires an entry drive off a certain street in order to make the internal circulation work properly, have your architect attempt to obtain written approval for the drive from the appropriate authorities before you buy.

If your site is not on a busy street, you may run into a different set of problems. It is possible to overtax the traffic capacity of the surrounding streets, usually to the dismay of the neighbors. You are left trying to maintain a delicate balance: the access streets must be neither too big nor too small. In real life, the access streets are seldom ideal.

INTERNAL CIRCULATION. The potential points of entry for your building site dictate much of the circulation within your site. Safety and convenience, in that order, are the primary goals for internal circulation. Libraries can generate quite a bit of traffic from all age groups. New parents pushing strollers, high-schoolers squealing the tires on their parents' cars, and retirees are all competing for space in the parking lot.

Other important considerations regarding internal site circulation include pedestrian routes from the parking lot to the building, access for emergency vehicles, and the accessibility of the site for the handicapped. Since the passage of the ADA, there are, for the first time, uniform federal design standards to ensure that all public sites are made accessible. All public buildings must conform to the standards set forth in the ADA.

BARRIERS. For building sites in hilly areas, accessibility can become a challenging issue. For example, suppose your building is on a hillside, with the building on the uphill side and the parking lot on the lower portion, 5 feet below the elevation of your main entry. A 5-foot difference in elevation, or 60 inches, doesn't seem like a terribly long climb. At the standard 7 inches maximum rise per stair, that's only nine steps. To accommodate a wheelchair, however, a 60-inch difference in elevation means 70 feet of wheelchair ramp, including two landings and possibly switchbacks in addition. Not only is the difference in elevation difficult for the wheelchair user to negotiate, it can be difficult for the architect and landscape architect to integrate the ramp into the site design.

☑ *Climate*

ORIENTATION. The *orientation* of a building is its placement with respect to the path of the sun and prevailing winds. In temperate climates, the rule of thumb is to place most of the windows facing north or south and to keep the west side free of too many openings that allow late afternoon sun to penetrate the building. Direct sunlight both increases electric bills for cooling the building and admits ultraviolet rays that can damage a library collection. To prevent direct sunlight from entering in the summer, overhangs or other sun-shading devices can be placed over south-facing windows to provide shade.

Each site also has special conditions that affect the desired placement and orientation of the building. Tall buildings on a neighboring property, a nearby grove of pine trees, or an adjacent lake must all be considered. Any of these features can modify

---

THE BOOK DROP DILEMMA

Most of our library clients ask that we provide a drive-up book drop. Some are book returns only; others feature a staffed window where patrons can pick up reserved books and conduct other library business. A drive-up book drop can have a significant impact on the design (and even selection) of your site. The smaller your library, the more the impact. Follow this logic:

> A drive-up book drop requires an access drive and generates additional vehicular traffic.
>
> Whenever possible, a drive-up book drop should bring books directly into the circulation work room.
>
> The circulation work room is usually near the circulation desk.
>
> The circulation desk is usually near the front entry of the library.
>
> Pedestrians enter the library via the front entry, which is near the circulation desk, which is near the circulation work room, which is near the book drop.

Conclusion: Drive-up book drops can wind up being near the entry to the library, which can put them in close proximity to pedestrians entering the building. In terms of site circulation, we try to avoid mixing cars and people. In that contest, the cars always win.

For a smaller library, where things already tend to be closer to each other because of the size of the building, a drive-up book drop can force cars and pedestrians to cross paths. One solution involves putting the book drop in a more remote location of the library (obviously less efficient, but doable), or altering the shape of the library to accommodate the drive-up and get the cars out of the way before they encounter the main entry. This can take up space, because of the turning radius requirements for automobile traffic. In any case, the existence of the book drop can force an increase in the overall size of the site and should be integrated into the site selection process.

what is known as the *microclimate* of a site. Program requirements must also be taken into account. A library with a large rare-book collection, for example, should be designed with few windows to minimize damage to the collection from the ultraviolet component of sunlight. A busy street might also be a reason to limit the number of openings on that face of the building, to keep down the noise level inside.

For every limitation, a building site offers an opportunity. Proper orientation of the building brings you the maximum benefit from your site. Visit the building site with your architect and landscape architect to discuss its qualities. Let them know what you think is important, what you want to see and hear, and what distractions you want to avoid.

☑ Landscaping

LANDSCAPE PLAN. The complete site design comes later in the project, but a complete site analysis can include at least a preliminary landscape plan. Landscaping addresses both aesthetic and practical considerations. Groundcovers can soften hard edges and define walkways. Well-placed trees provide shade, guide pedestrian circulation, and enhance your building at the same time. Flowers add beauty and can direct attention to selected site elements like signs or entries. Many aspects of landscape design are significant in sustainable building design (see chapter 13).

The landscape architect also uses many nonplant materials to achieve desired effects. Railroad ties might retain soil in a planting area; bark chips could define a path to an outdoor area for children's programs. Re-creations of antique lamp posts might be used to provide exterior lighting if your library is in a historic neighborhood. Local stone might provide an interesting material for walls and planters.

A good landscape plan adds a softer, human touch to your building. Though it may seem expensive at the time, investing in trees and other landscape materials pays back impressive dividends as the plants mature. The importance of exterior terraces, walks, and screens should also be considered. An added advantage to landscaping is that it can often increase the energy efficiency of your building. During summer months in temperate climates, deciduous trees can provide shade and effectively reduce your cooling costs. In winter months the leaves have fallen and sunshine warms and brightens the interior spaces. Coniferous trees on the north and west sides protect against both winter winds and late afternoon summer sun, which can otherwise increase air conditioning costs.

In northeastern Illinois where I live, suburbs are expanding around Chicago and new housing developments dot the landscape. These places all seem to have one thing in common: last week they were cornfields. After driving through interchangeable subdivisions with their endless chemically greened lawns, I am always relieved to get back to my 1905 farmhouse, where mature trees line the roads and the results of one hundred years worth of weekend yard projects blend into a rich and varied mixture. Remember that your building is going to be there for a long time, easily long enough for an ambitious landscape plan to mature.

☑ No library is an island

OUTDOOR SPACES. Unless it is particularly tight, a building site offers a lot more than a place to set a building and parking lot. A hillside or berm might be sculpted to provide a seating area for children during a storytelling or musical program; a nature walk could be designed and plants selected to illustrate the changing of the seasons to grade-schoolers. Butterfly gardens, with plants specially selected to appeal to different species of butterflies and moths, can be planted where they are visible from reading areas. You and your architect can explore such opportunities during the site design.

At my firm, our library design team employs the concept that "no library is an island." Essentially, we believe that there are many ways a library can relate to its site and the surrounding community. It's no news to the library professional that the mission of libraries has expanded well beyond the traditional model of a place to store books and find access to reference services.

We recently designed a large addition for the Wheaton (Illinois) Public Library. The finished project resulted in a library with a floor area something over 110,000 square feet. Since its initial construction in the 1960s, the library was across the street from a one-square-block city park. During the design phase, we reasoned that the library and the park could do more for each other than just being neighbors. We researched the street separating the park from the library and found out that it had no major utilities running under it, and that the traffic count was low. We ran the idea of merging the library and park past the library board, who thought it was a good idea. Only half believing that the city council would go for it, we petitioned them to close the street for that block so we could unite the library and the park. The council approved the concept, and the street was closed.

Rather than merely remove the street, we looked for additional ways the library could interact with the park and the community. In place of the street we provided a pedestrian way with paving bricks and landscaping to provide a transition to the park. We provided areas specifically designed to accommodate farmers' markets, art shows, exhibitions, concerts, and other public events. Whether the library or some other entity hosts an event there is unimportant; the goal is to get more people to the library and to make the library into a community center. In the scheme of the overall project, the pedestrian way was not an expensive exercise. For a very reasonable price, the library gained all sorts of additional ways to interact with the community. This library will not be an island. In site design as well as building design, you and your architect should look at all aspects of the project and ask yourselves, What more can this be?

> ### THERE, THERE
>
> Speaking of Oakland, California, Gertrude Stein said, "There is no *there* there." I feel much the same in those anonymous suburbs. Landscaping is one of the things that can transform a building site into a place. Whether your library is modest or grand, it deserves a place.

What the Architect Should Give You

At the end of the site analysis phase of a project, your architect should present the results of the analysis to the board and the management staff. Much of the site analysis is presented in graphic form. The architect, armed with display boards and pointer, may appear before the board to make the presentation and to answer questions.

The presentation boards should illustrate the site with an assumed building footprint superimposed on it. I say "assumed" because, at this early stage of the design, the shape of the building has not been completely defined. Traffic flow and parking should be indicated, as should surrounding streets. Topography is often shown along with the site drainage patterns.

Building setbacks, easements, and rights-of-way may be shown on the presentation boards; these graphic interpretations of the site limitations greatly aid understanding the possibilities of your site. Significant vegetation and other landscape features should also be illustrated, for they will have a great impact on the placement and orientation of your building.

Specialized site plans may also be presented. Some may show only soil conditions, to illustrate which portions of the site are buildable; others may illustrate the extent of wetlands or floodplains. Opportunities for views and adjacent land uses also may be shown. Of course, the number of plans presented and the extent of the information they cover depend entirely on your own circumstances. A building addition usually needs only a minimum amount of site analysis; a cluster of new buildings on a large site might require a master plan as well as smaller-scale site analyses. The graphic material provided by the architect can also be used as presentation materials for public inspection as part of a referendum campaign.

Some written information might also be presented. Soil reports, surveys, and a verbal summary of the site analysis are often bound into a report. The large presentation boards can be reduced and included in the report to provide a complete site analysis document at a manageable size.

Sign-Off

In previous chapters I indicated that I recommend a formal sign-off at the end of each phase of the project. Have the architect include a formal sign-off sheet at the end of the program analysis documents. The board members and library director should sign this page to indicate their formal acceptance of the site analysis and their approval of the completed work and the direction of the project. Their signatures indicate the end of the site analysis phase and confirm that any additional site analysis work they request of the architect may result in a request for additional compensation. If the architect has not produced all the items that were previously agreed on, the board should discuss the matter with the architect. It may turn out that some of the services agreed to were not applicable to the site in question. Usually a brief discussion can resolve these questions to the satisfaction of the board, and either the board will sign the document or the architect will be directed to produce the remaining items before the sign-off is completed.

Building Design

If you ask many people what an architect does, the answer is often something to the effect of "design buildings." Although architects spend much of their time performing other tasks, design remains the heart of the profession. Design has an impact on us all. Almost anyone could probably name an example of a building they find particularly pleasing, bad, or inappropriate.

Many forms of art are experienced in a fleeting fashion, during a walk past a sculpture on a downtown plaza or perhaps on an annual visit to an art museum. But a building is a work of art in which you live and work. Granted, it's not necessarily a significant artwork, but countless design decisions are made in planning even the simplest and most utilitarian of buildings. Of course, there are exceptions to every rule; it is difficult to find the spark of creativity in the prefabricated metal buildings that are now replacing old barns across America, and some utilitarian structures like telephone switching stations are virtually nothing more than brick or metal-clad boxes. That doesn't have to be the case.

Of Buildings and Boxes

I recently read of the impending demolition of an old electrical substation near where I live. This building wasn't significant in a design sense, but it was pleasing. Arched windows, nice brickwork, and considered proportions lent it a grace lacking in many of the newer buildings that surrounded it. You could tell that this building, as simple as it was, was designed. Someone had thought about it. In contrast, some of its more recent cousins appear to have been *installed* rather than designed. For a period of time culminating in the 1960s, there was movement toward eliminating what was perceived to be "unnecessary" and "applied" detail on buildings. In the hands of a master architect like Mies van der Rohe, this style found form in some powerful and elegant buildings that are landmarks in recent architectural history. In the hands of others, it resulted in swarms of buildings that were little more than boxes; some were glass, some were brick, some were metal, some were stone, some were combinations of materials, but all were still boxes.

This look was so sought after that many turn-of-the-century buildings on small town main streets were "modernized" by covering them with painted metal panels to make them appear to be closer to the ideal of the box. Perhaps the goal was to have entire cities that looked installed rather than designed. The results, however, never looked as "clean" as their makers intended; they were invariably cluttered with things like street numbers, which were becoming more necessary than ever in order to tell the buildings apart.

We seem to have at least temporarily outgrown the need to cover up what is old; indeed, an older building is now often perceived as a status symbol. Rehabilitating old warehouses and industrial buildings for upscale clients is a current vogue, although the results aren't necessarily any more imaginative or successful than the boxes of a few decades ago. Reuse of old buildings is accepted as valid strategy in sustainable architecture. When I discuss sustainability in chapter 13, we explore some of the benefits and pitfalls of reusing existing buildings as libraries.

> *It shall be framed upon a single, noble motive, to which the design of all its parts, in some more or less subtle way, shall be confluent and helpful.*
>
> —Frederick Olmstead

> *The physician can bury his mistakes, but the architect can only advise his clients to plant vines.*
>
> —Frank Lloyd Wright

Compromise, Creativity, and Gary Cooper

In doing research for this book, I read everything I could lay my hands on concerning the practice of architecture and the nature of the architect/client relationship. I even went to my local library and checked out a DVD of *The Fountainhead,* the 1949 film version of Ayn Rand's book in which Gary Cooper plays Howard Roark, an idealistic young architect fighting a personal battle to avoid compromising his principles in order to merely please the crowd.

I jumped at the chance to see him play the role of the heroic, misunderstood yet brilliant architect. I could really identify with this character. Please forgive me if I summarize the plot for those who haven't read the book or seen the film.

In the film, Howard Roark suffers a series of career setbacks. To make ends meet, he is forced to allow another architect to use one of his designs for a building. The other architect yields to business pressures and allows the design to be changed to make it more in keeping with the client's idea of what the public really wants. Howard is so upset by this affront to his design sensibilities that he goes to the site and dynamites the partially completed building. The client is understandably upset by this turn of events and insists on legal action. After an impassioned courtroom speech in which Howard takes the jury from the discovery of fire to the advent of totalitarianism (remember, this is 1949), a "not guilty" verdict is returned. The rights of the individual are upheld and the prerogative of the designer is protected. Somehow, the client's right to get what he was paying for was left out of the equation. The movie guidebook on my bookshelf generously awards *The Fountainhead* two and a half stars.

In actual practice, architects hardly ever blow up buildings they don't like. An impromptu poll of my peers turned up no one who would admit doing so.

Howard Roark would attest to the fact that design is the most emotionally charged part of a project. While designing, architects must seek the balance between their creative impulses and the practical needs of their clients. Architecture is art that solves problems. To a degree, compromise is always part of the process. Buildings must conform to the site. Budgetary realities have to be recognized, and the wishes of the client must be taken into consideration. A successful design addresses those limitations and transcends them. Your part in the design process is to work with your architect and foster the working relationship.

The quality of the relationship between client and architect has a great impact on the design process. Some clients want a lot of involvement and may wish to have a say in all but the most minor of design decisions. Others may want only broad oversight of the architect's work and may be content to see the design only at certain milestone points. Sometimes the project is handed to the architect, who then has carte blanche to solve the problems as he or she sees fit, as long as the final result conforms to the budget and program requirements. Most projects are of the second type; the design proceeds and is reviewed by the client at certain, predetermined times. This is probably the most efficient method. It frees the architect and the client from constant meetings dealing with project minutiae yet provides enough oversight to reduce the chances of a major redrawing of the plans when the design is finally presented. For most of our library work, we maintain an intense involvement with the library director and staff throughout the design phase, whereas check-ins with library trustees are limited to monthly updates at board or design committee meetings.

Building design is typically broken up into two phases—schematic design and design development. Each phase requires specific things from the architect and the client. A good understanding of the design process enables you to get the greatest benefit from your architect and helps ensure you get the product you want.

Schematic Design

Schematic design can be a little difficult to separate from design development, for in some ways the distinction is arbitrary. Design is a process that continues throughout the project, from programming through construction. Separating design into two phases is convenient in terms of the architect's billing for professional services and helps ensure adequate client involvement during the design phase by offering a predetermined milestone point for review of the design. Schematic design usually represents approximately 15 percent of the architect's fee.

What the Architect Does

In schematic design the architect begins with the building program and site analysis that were produced during predesign and approved by the client. Schematic design represents the first effort to determine the relative sizes and relationships of the elements defined in the building program. The prime objective is to arrive at a clearly defined, feasible concept and to present it in a form that is understandable to the client. The secondary objectives are to clarify the building program, explore the most promising alternative design solutions, and develop a reliable basis for estimating the cost of the project.

Many aspects of the design and general philosophy are discussed with the client during the schematic design phase. This is the time when many of the major decisions regarding the basic plan and look of your building are made. The overall concept behind the building design, sometimes called the "big idea," is generated and reviewed with the client. The big idea may take the form of a simple and somewhat abstract phrase like "a circle within a square," or it can take the form of a quick, conceptual sketch based on a single, strong form like a major axis with radiating branches. Sometimes it may be a verbally expressed concept like "no library is an island." Whatever form it takes, the overall concept is an ordering mechanism for the architect and offers a point of beginning. It is intended to narrow the range of solutions being explored and gives the project direction.

Rough designs now begin to be developed. At this point, they may still take the form of bubble diagrams, but the relative sizes of the bubbles are adjusted to begin to correspond to the relative sizes of the spaces they represent. Many alternative solutions may be drawn. As the solutions are refined and reviewed with the client, some of them are dropped and the field becomes limited to just a few of the most promising ones.

The project schedule is refined at this time. Though long-term schedules can be difficult to keep, they are important in monitoring the progress of the work. The architect should keep the board apprised of any changes to the schedule as the project commences.

At the close of schematic design the architect usually makes a formal presentation to the board. There should be few surprises if everyone has been involved in the process. The formal presentation is often made at a board meeting, thus giving the public and the media their first opportunity to see what's in store for the library.

What the Board Should Do

The board should be active in the schematic design so that that the project evolves according to their wishes. At the start of the schematic design phase, several meetings should be scheduled with the architect. These meetings need not be formal presentations, but at the very least the architect should show the board what design options are being considered and be able to state the rationale behind each of them.

Take the time to study each of the proposed solutions and be prepared to voice any concerns during the review meetings. It is best that your comments be delivered to the architect before the entire board, so that each may know where the others stand. It is vitally important to build a board consensus during schematic design, for subsequent changes can be expensive and could affect the project schedule.

Initial cost estimates should be scrutinized, shared with financial consultants and the library's legal counsel, and evaluated against the available funds. During schematic design it sometimes becomes apparent that the project cannot be built with the available funding. In this case, either additional funding must be sought, the architect must fit the program into a more efficient, cost-effective package, or the building program must trimmed to bring the project within budget. This harkens back to the "hard decisions" we discussed in chapter 4. If the program must be cut significantly, extra meetings should be called with the project team and architect to reach a resolution.

CUT 'EM SOME SLACK

Leave architects room to do their job. Sometimes clients approach an architect to do a project with set, preconceived ideas—sometimes expressed as, "We know exactly what we want, and all you have to do is draw it." This is a good news–bad news proposition for the architect. The good news is that the clients have probably already given a lot of thought to their project and may have a clear idea of their needs. The bad news is that some of their ideas may be inappropriate in the larger context of the program, the site analysis, building codes, affordability, and the like. Let the architect know your concepts for the building, but try to maintain an open mind if the schematic designs the architect produces do not exactly fit your ideas. Remember that you are paying for the architect's expertise. To get the most for your money, don't maintain too tight a rein.

Ask your building engineer to review the architect's recommendations for mechanical, electrical, and plumbing systems to verify that the types of equipment proposed are within the capabilities of your staff to operate and maintain. As the demand for energy efficiency increases, so does the complexity of the systems that are going into today's buildings. Sometimes training seminars are offered by the companies that manufacture the equipment. If the new systems are significantly more complicated than the old, ask your engineer to explore the avenues for additional training. This is especially important in the case of complex mechanical control systems. I recently ran into a case where a library's engineer had been operating a digital building control system incorrectly since the building was completed. For years, building occupants complained of being too hot in one part of the building and too cold in another part. It took our mechanical engineer all of two hours to reprogram the system and remedy what had been nearly a decade of poor performance. We take this up again when we discuss building commissioning in chapter 13.

Ask the architect to propose a schedule for the design and construction of the building. Evaluate the schedule in light of your needs. Architects have every incentive to get their portion of the work completed as soon as possible; in most cases, the longer a job drags on, the less the architect makes per hour of effort. If the estimate for the project construction time exceeds your timetable, discuss ways to speed up the process with your architect. There are alternatives like fast-track construction which, for a price, make things happen faster.

AN EYE TOWARD THE FUTURE

There is one aspect of building design that you should insist on: making accommodations for future expansion. Ask the architect to provide an avenue for expanding your building should it ever become necessary. Having the flexibility to be able to add on to your building (and parking) later could well save some future building committee from facing the prospect of relocating in order to accommodate expanding library needs. Even if you do wind up relocating, having the potential for expansion often means that your building will command a higher selling price. It is usually a good move to leave yourself some options. On library projects that have a near-term need (within a decade or so) for expansion, we prefer to produce a second schematic design that includes the future work to illustrate just how the building can be expanded. This is a valuable exercise that ensures that there is a rational plan for expanding the library in the future. We charge the client for the additional schematic design but feel it is well worth it in the long run. Many building plans have nothing more than a dotted line delineating the area slated for future construction. Unless a real plan is worked out ahead of time, this approach can be useless or even misleading. Roof lines, mechanical systems, foundation systems, and elevations need to be defined in a schematic form to prove that the future plans are realistic.

CHANGES

If the board requests significant changes to the schematic design at one of the review points, make sure that the request is given to the architect in written form; meeting minutes usually suffice. This is done to help reduce the chances of any misunderstandings regarding the board's wishes and to have a written record of the course of the project.

It is important that your internal chain of command be defined and in place. The architect should have a set way of receiving instructions regarding changes to the work. I have seen many cases where an architect made revisions to a project only to discover later that the person asking for the changes had no real authority to do so. Sometimes a board member contacts the architect directly, asking for some feature without the rest of the board's knowledge. The end result can be a partial redraw, bad feelings within the project team, and possibly a request for additional fees on the part of the architect. For the outsider, it is not always obvious who has the authority in your organization. Sit down with the architect at the beginning of the project and work out how instructions are to be transmitted. In the case of a public library, written instructions signed by the library director or board president may be required.

Finally, the end of schematic design represents another milestone point in your project. The board should again sign off on each item presented to indicate their acceptance of the work done to date.

What the Architect Should Give You

After the schematic design phase of a project is completed, the client can typically expect to have one or more conceptual building designs in hand. At this stage of the project, these design solutions may even be freehand drawings. They are not intended to show the exact sizes and placement of all the parts of the building; rather, they express the building program information graphically.

Schematic cost estimates are also typically generated at this time. As the building begins to take shape, the accuracy of the estimated prices begins to increase. Many architects use professional price estimators. If you are using a small to medium-size architectural firm, chances are that it does not have a professional estimator on staff. I advise library boards to encourage the architect to retain an independent estimator to give detailed cost estimates at several points during the project. Detailed estimating is usually an additional service, but it can pay off in terms of a smooth-running project.

Before we go any farther, let's talk about costs.

COST ESTIMATES ARE JUST THAT

Throughout the project someone, somewhere, should be preparing estimates for the ultimate cost of the project and sharing those estimates with the client. Cost estimating lies somewhere between art and science. An experienced estimator has a database of information with cost histories for everything likely to go into your building. In addition to material costs the estimator has an understanding of different construction systems as well as local labor rates. We prefer to use independent, professional cost estimators for detailed estimates rather than do the estimates in-house. Our reasoning is that an architect is seldom as good at estimating as a person who estimates full time. That being said, one must always remember that an estimator is trying to predict the future.

Anyone can ensure that a project will come in under budget by padding the initial estimate enough. The art of estimating is knowing just how much to include to account for the unknown. If the estimates are padded too much, the project eventually comes in substantially under budget. This sounds great until you realize that your building could have been bigger or you could have included features that were dropped because of cost concerns.

We recently had a project that was estimated and went to a public referendum for funding. The referendum was approved by the voters and our clients were thrilled—they were going to get their new library. Remember that referenda deliver a set amount of project funding, and that a project must be adjusted as required to fit within that funding. If the estimating is on track everything is fine, but . . .

Just as the drawings were completed and the projects slated to go out to bid, this country experienced some devastating Gulf Coast hurricanes. Overnight, the costs of lumber and gypsum board increased. Everything got more expensive as resources were diverted to the rebuilding effort. On top of that, China's economy was starting to heat up. Competition with China for structural steel was increasing, and the price of steel rose significantly. All of this happened after the estimates were completed and the referendum was held. Things didn't look good.

THE IMPORTANCE OF CONTINGENCY

The way to protect your project from the unexpected is to include a contingency fund in the project budget. This is an amount added to the expected cost of a project to account for inflation and unexpected conditions. Every project has its share of unexpected events. In construction, unexpected events almost never reduce the cost of the building. Contingency should be included in every phase of the project. The general rule is that, the earlier it is in the project or the more complex the project is, the higher the contingency should be. Our first initial estimates may include contingency numbers of up to 15 percent of the cost of construction. By the end of the design development phase, the contingency may be down to 10 percent. Usually, 5 percent is reserved as "design contingency" to account for late-breaking design changes, and 5 percent is reserved for the construction phase to account for the inevitable surprises that crop up on any construction project. In the United States, the average building usually increases 3–5 percent during the construction phase because of design changes and unforeseen conditions.

What happened with our project after weathering hurricanes and international competition? Our estimator had foreseen the likelihood of the Chinese economy on the price of steel and increased the initial contingency from 15 to 18 percent. I remember complaining about it at the time; after all, it was making us cut back on features we wanted. His foresight decreased the impact of the steel cost increases but did not fully make up for the hurricane-related inflation. The client found a little more money; interest rates were up, and the bonds were earning more than originally anticipated. We also cut back on the design a bit, and eventually the project was brought in on budget, albeit a little smaller than originally anticipated. Things came out all right in the end, even if the process was a little painful. Without the contingency, it would have been a disaster.

CHECKLIST OF SCHEMATIC DESIGN ELEMENTS

☑ *Small-scale floor plans*

Floor plans are included in the schematic design presentation. Depending on the project, they may be little more than bubble diagrams drawn to scale, or they may be recognizable floor plans at a small scale—usually at $\frac{1}{16}$ inch equals 1 foot. This small scale keeps the level of detail to a minimum and reflects the degree of refinement of the design at this point.

☑ *Building elevations*

Building elevations (straight-on views of each face of the building) should be included. Note that elevations can be misleading. Since they are drawn without perspective, parts of the building that are more distant from the viewing position are not drawn smaller than nearer parts of the building. Because of this, it can be difficult for a nonarchitect to interpret elevations.

☑ *Building sections*

One or two building sections should be included; these may be at the same small scale as the floor plans. A building section depicts an imaginary slice made vertically through the building and illustrates the relationship of foundations, floors, ceilings, mechanical spaces, and roofs.

☑ *Site plan*

A schematic site plan should show the building placement, parking lots, anticipated site circulation, and major landscape features. As with the building floor plans, the site plan may be drawn at a small scale.

☑ *Outline specification*

The specification is a written document that sets the standards of quality for the construction, names acceptable products and materials, and itemizes additional responsibilities of the contractor. An outline specification is a very general description of the work; it gives a broad overview of building systems and materials and is used by the cost estimator for the schematic estimate.

☑ *Preliminary estimates of construction cost*

Whether or not a professional estimator is utilized, an estimated construction cost should be furnished. Contingencies of at least 10 percent should be included to cover unanticipated conditions.

☑ *Documentation of mechanical, electrical, and plumbing systems*

During schematic design the architect begins to coordinate the work of the various other professionals who will contribute to the project. The schematic design should have, at a minimum, written descriptions of the mechanical and electrical systems being considered for the building. The preliminary design of these systems is an important part of early planning and is required for accurate, early estimates of the construction cost.

☑ *Renderings*

You may wish to obtain renderings for use as promotional tools. They can be displayed in the lobby to stimulate public interest and taken to those Rotary Club meetings to add a little visual interest while you are plugging your referendum. Artistic renderings are usually considered to be an additional service.

☑ *Other services*

Your architect can supply you with any number of other services tailored to your project. Detailed life-cycle cost analyses, models, promotional materials, and energy use studies are a few of the services you could consider. Another potential service is marketing.

MARKETING

At the close of the schematic design phase you have a reasonably good idea of what your building will look like, how it will work, and roughly how much it will cost. In the project checklist presented above, I mentioned the marketing potential of renderings with respect to fund-raising. The information collected and the designs generated during schematic design can be powerful marketing tools. People love visual aids. Appropriate renderings can generate excitement for your project. A model of the planned project is always a popular display. Renderings and models can be expensive, but nothing beats them if you need to get your message across in an effective manner. With computer-aided design, it is now possible to produce startlingly lifelike representations of buildings and outdoor spaces for display on a video screen or reproduction as color photographs. These can even be animated to give the impression of a walk through the still-imaginary building. Generally, the more detailed the rendering, the more it costs. Lifelike, animated walk-throughs are particularly expensive, since they require the architect to design and render more of the interior than might otherwise be the case at this stage of the project.

The reason I mention marketing now is that the close of the schematic design phase can be a logical point to pause for fund-raising. With available cost figures and the potential for some impressive visual presentations, you have a lot more to show than you did at the beginning of the project. Sometimes an institution retains an architect on a two-phase basis. The contract might be written so that the project proceeds beyond the schematic design phase only if the fund-raising effort is successful. In this manner the library is not paying for additional architectural services it won't need if the funding is not forthcoming. Indeed, if a fully completed architectural project were to sit on the shelf for several years awaiting funding, the drawings might have to be modified to account for changes in program, equipment, or building codes that might have occurred in the interim.

This two-phase approach to the architectural project also serves to add a potentially powerful fund-raiser to your team—the architect. Architects tend to be involved in their communities. Some of them, because of the nature of their work, are accomplished public speakers. If the board members are making the rounds of the service club lunches, the architect might be asked to come along to help field questions. This gets into the potentially sensitive area of asking the architect to provide what might be pro bono services. If a two-phase effort is being considered, discuss this with the architect, who may be willing to toss a few of these kinds of appearances in for free, or on an hourly rate. Either way, the potential for the architect to serve as a salesperson should not be overlooked. After all, they wouldn't have the job if they hadn't sold you.

Design Development

When the schematic design is complete and has been approved by all participants, the project can proceed into the design development phase. The goal of design development is to refine and elaborate on the design that was produced during the schematic design phase. Now you begin to see your building take shape. Many of the major decisions may have been made, but there is a lot of input that you, as client, are still expected to provide. This is an exciting time, and your building committee will be kept busy in numerous meetings with the architect as design ideas are presented and discussed.

What the Architect Does

During design development the architect begins to define the details of the project. The structural system, mechanical and electrical systems, and site design are developed. Floor plans are drawn that show spaces and program elements in scale and in accurate relationships. Drawings are developed that illustrate the exterior appearance of the building to a greater level of detail than was generated during the schematic design. On a typical project the design development phase represents 15–20 percent of the architect's contract.

The outline specification is also expanded, and more selections of materials and types of construction are made. Room finishes and lighting systems are defined. The board and library director should be familiar with these choices and take an active part in the selection process. The interior finishes will determine to a large extent the "feel" of your library. The outline specifications also include general information regarding the electrical and mechanical systems of the building. Again, your building engineer should be involved in the review of proposed mechanical and electrical systems.

At this stage of the project, the architect is actively coordinating the work of numerous consultants who are contributing to the evolution of the building. Scale drawings are produced by the structural, electrical, mechanical, and plumbing engineers to ensure that the systems for which they are responsible are integrated into the overall building design. A lot of the architect's time goes into the coordination of the consultants. This coordination is essential to ensure against time-consuming and potentially costly changes later in the project. The building engineer should be made a part of this process to represent the library and verify that decisions made regarding building systems are consistent with the ideas that were defined in the schematic design.

The set of drawings the architect has been working on now begin to grow as additional sheets for the structural and mechanical systems are included. Up to this point, the layperson could pick up the drawings and understand pretty much what was being indicated on each sheet. The information now being included by the structural and mechanical consultants is more esoteric. Few board members can look at a heating and ventilating sheet or electrical drawing and get a real feel for what's going on. As the architect gives you progressive sets of drawings, take a little time to review them. Note any questions, and don't be afraid to ask them during review meetings. As the advertising slogan goes, "An informed consumer is our best customer." As a trustee of someone else's money, it is your duty to be that "informed consumer."

What the Board Should Do

The board's responsibilities during design development resemble those of the schematic design phase. Your primary duty is to maintain an active role by reviewing and commenting on the architect's work. As before, set up a regular series of meetings so the architect may present progressive sets showing the progress of the work to date. Be prepared to have several special meetings between the architect and the building committee to discuss detailed questions. All decisions made at these meetings should be written and transmitted to the board for review at the next full board meeting.

As the design development proceeds, review the building goals that were identified back during the programming phase. It is easy to get so involved with the day-to-day progress of your project that you lose sight of the original goals. Programs should be dusted off and examined from time to time to verify that the project is proceeding in conformance with them. They may have to be revised somewhat in light of what you've learned since then. If so, revise them in a formal manner at a board meeting and record significant changes. As an aside, we often find that the client's recollection of what is in their building program fades in the interval between building programming and design. As the design progresses and the drawings begin to take shape, there are always a few instances of "I don't remember asking for that" or "Who put that in the program?" Building programs are not immutable; they evolve as the project progresses. The degree to which you attain your goals is one of the yardsticks by which you can evaluate the success of your building and the performance of your architect. When evaluating the success of your project, don't lose sight of the fact that programs represent an ultimate goal and may not take feasibility into account. The percentage of the program that is actually achieved by the design is influenced by financial considerations, the size of the building site, and a host of other factors.

At the close of the design development phase, the architect usually makes a presentation to the board to secure formal approval of the material produced. The board should again formally indicate their acceptance by signing off on the work.

What the Architect Should Give You

At the end of the design development phase you will have a complete building design. Floor plans, elevations, site plans, and landscape plans are all drawn to scale. Materials are indicated and the various structural and mechanical systems are shown. At the client's request, a detailed estimate of the construction cost can be produced at this time. I recommend asking the architect to involve a professional cost consultant to help improve the accuracy of the cost estimate.

The design development submittal should include the following documents:

☑ Architectural floor plans

Floor plans should be provided for all areas of the building. The scale of these plans is larger than that for the schematic design plans. For most buildings, the scale should be at least ⅛ inch equals 1 foot. Larger-scale (¼ inch = 1 foot) detailed plans may be given for areas of particular complexity or importance. Walls should be indicated with their appropriate thicknesses, and door swings should be drawn.

The structural grid system should be developed and shown on the plans. The structural grid is a system of intersecting lines that intersect at column locations; this allows each column to be defined by a particular grid position (e.g., Column A-7). Built-in casework and built-in equipment should also be indicated at this time. If your architect lacks library experience, make sure the spacing of book stacks has been taken into account in the laying out of the column grid. Inappropriately spaced columns can significantly reduce the efficiency of a library.

☑ Reflected ceiling plans

Reflected ceiling plans show the construction of the ceiling as if it is being looked down on from above. They show the layout of ceiling tile grid systems (if any), ceiling details, and the locations of light fixtures, ventilation grilles, and sprinkler heads.

☑ Interior elevations

Detailed interior elevations are produced at a later stage. At this point there may be only a few to illustrate some of the more important interior spaces. The interior elevations illustrate the appearance of doors, windows, casework, and other interior detailing. Only built-in items are shown; moveable equipment and furniture are typically omitted.

☑ *Building elevations*

Building elevations are included, with finish materials indicated and vertical dimensions shown. Windows and doors should be drawn to represent the appearance of the selected items. The scale of these drawings is usually the same as that of the floor plans. Roof structures, including mechanical equipment, should be indicated. Larger-scale partial elevations should be given for particularly important or complex areas.

☑ *Building sections*

Building sections are shown with greater detail than those given on the schematic design documents. Spaces for ducts should be indicated, as should floor levels and suspended ceilings. The building sections are particularly important in enhancing your understanding of the building, and they should be studied closely.

☑ *Construction details*

Some of the construction details that are most important in establishing the building's character may be included. These could be typical wall sections, parapets, window details, stair details, construction details for interior partitions, or custom millwork items.

☑ *Site plan*

A site plan should show the building placement, parking lots, anticipated site circulation, and major landscape features. Easements and rights-of-way should be indicated, as should civil engineering items such as sewers, fire hydrants, and manholes. The plan should show the proposed grading scheme, landscaping, and site lighting plan.

☑ *Outline specification*

The specification is developed to a greater degree of detail than for the schematic design phase. Selections for major construction and finish materials should be included.

☑ *Estimates of construction cost*

The estimated construction cost should show line item costs for various building components such as foundations, structural systems, finishes, plumbing, and electrical systems. Significant contingencies should still be included to cover unanticipated conditions and changes. The contingencies can be reduced somewhat as the design is developed.

☑ *Structural plans and details*

A general indication of the structural plan of the building might be included. These drawings should be carefully coordinated with the architectural sheets.

☑ *Mechanical, electrical, and plumbing plans and details*

Some information regarding the mechanical, electrical, and plumbing systems might be included. These sections illustrate the construction of their respective systems. Coordination with the architectural sheets is again of primary importance in assuring a successful project.

☑ *Renderings*

As with schematic design, artistic renderings are not usually considered a basic service. Include them in the architect's contract as an extra if you wish.

☑ *Additional services*

The list of potential additional services is much the same as those we covered in schematic design. Probably the most significant addition is interior design. Interior furnishings and color selections are often not part of the scope of the architect's work. Many clients retain the architect to design the interiors; others hire an interior designer. If you hire an interior designer, have several joint meetings with both the architect and the interior designer to make sure they have a compatible understanding of the project and its goals. Library design is a specialty. Utilizing an interior designer with experience in library design will facilitate the process.

✧ ✧ ✧

The two checklists presented in this chapter are not intended to be exhaustive or universal. Each project is unique, and each architect is different. If the design development site plan does not include site lighting, don't automatically assume that you are getting an inferior product and ask for your money back. If the set is lacking something you feel is particularly important to your project, you can ask the architect to add it to the set and delay the formal acceptance of the design development documents until they are done to your satisfaction—up to a point.

Talk Softly, but Carry a Signed Contract

If the board rejects an architect's submittal as incomplete and requests additional information, it is important to be sure that the services being requested are included in the architect's scope of work as stated in the original agreement between client and architect. There are occasional stories of architects providing services at the request of their clients and then, after the fact, submitting an invoice for additional fees for services not included in their contract. There are other instances where clients refuse to pay the architect for services already rendered unless the architect provides additional work at no charge. Both scenarios could represent either unethical behavior or merely poor communications between client and architect. An architect should always inform the client in writing if services are being requested that will result in a change to the contract amount. A client should always be aware of the scope of services included in the contract and expect to pay more for additional services. Maintaining a good architect/client relationship implies a degree of trust in the professional conduct of both parties.

Construction Documents

In some ways a building is like an intricate machine composed of tens of thousands of parts. Somewhere, at some time, each of those parts was chosen to satisfy a particular need. The size of every steel bolt was determined by the load it was to carry. The horsepower of each fan motor in the ventilation system was selected by the volume of air it would be expected to push through the ducts in a given time. The paint on the walls was chosen to be resistant to scuffing and have good covering ability. The spacing of the balusters along a stairway was designed so that a child's head would not fit between them.

Windows, Beams, and Bricks

Some of the parts that make up a building move; some are static. Some of them are seen, others hidden. The important point is that they all have to work together. Windows that are fabricated in Iowa must arrive at the site and fit into the openings the carpenters have made for them. A steel beam from Pennsylvania has to arrive already cut to the proper length and with holes predrilled in just the right places so it can take its intended place in the structural frame of the building. Caulk from Illinois has to be delivered in the proper color to match bricks that are being made in Colorado. Electronic control systems from California must be compatible with rooftop heating units made in Georgia. Thousands of relationships must be worked out and set to paper.

Other kinds of relationships must also be defined. Who is responsible for cleaning up the project site during construction? Who provides the surveys of the site? Who certifies that work is done according to the project specifications before a contractor's request for payment is honored? Who specifies how much insurance a contractor must carry to be able to bid on the work?

A building is a one-of-a-kind machine, made to order for a particular purpose. The written and graphic materials that define the relationships, requirements, and standards by which the project is to be constructed are known as the *construction documents*. The preparation of these documents is the responsibility of the architect, who, with the assistance of the client and the architect's consultants, puts together a set of documents that enable the construction of the building planned during design development. A well-prepared set of construction documents answers questions that are likely to come up from any quarter and ensures that the building will, like a well-designed machine, keep on running.

What the Architect Does

The construction documents phase of the project is the most labor-intensive and time-consuming phase for the architect. On a typical project this phase represents approximately 40 percent of the architect's contract. Once the design generated during the design development phase has been approved, the architect can prepare the drawings and specifications that set the requirements for the construction of the project.

The construction drawings show in graphic and written form the extent, design, locations, and relationships of the work to be done. Exact dimensions are worked out to ensure that the building "comes together." The drawings the architect puts together include those described in chapter 6 as well as numerous others required to describe the building adequately. They include floor plans, elevations, building sections, and site plans as well as details, diagrams, and schedules. During the construction documents phase, the architect continues to coordinate the work of the other consultants. The consultants each produce drawings and specifications to a similar level of detail as those produced by the architect. These drawings are assembled into a set which, along with the written specifications, forms the construction documents and provides contractors with the information they need to bid and build the project.

As a part of the construction documents phase, the project's legal framework is also defined. Contract forms are reviewed with the client and added to the construction documents package. Information in the contracts, specifications, bid forms, and drawings sets forth the legal rights and responsibilities of the client, the contractor, and the architect. At the end of the construction documents phase, the client has a complete package of documents that enable the project to be bid and built.

The architect now meets with the board and library staff to decide about equipment, materials, and contract details and guides this process by offering advice based on personal experience.

Dollars and Hours

Many clients are startled at the amount of time that goes into a set of construction documents. I've already mentioned that construction documents represent about 40 percent of the architect's contract, but how does that translate into hours? More important, what does that mean in dollars?

All projects are different, and there is a wide disparity between different architectural firms and between what architects get paid in different parts of the country. We can use the drawings portion of the contract documents as an example. In trying to determine fees, some architects use an average of 40–60 hours of drawing time to produce a sheet of working drawings. Some sheets have less detail and go quickly; some are complex and take more time. A medium-size library project might have twenty to thirty sheets of architectural drawings. If we use an average of 50 hours per sheet, that amounts to twenty-five to thirty-five full workweeks to produce the architectural drawings alone, not counting additional design time, specifications, and all the other sheets that must be produced by the architect's consultants. If we assume an average billing rate of $120 an hour for an architect, the cost could be in the range of $175,000 for the architect's portion of the drawings, which does not include the drawings produced by all the other consultants.

I discuss fees in more detail in chapter 11, but I mention them now to give an indication of the investment the architect and board have in the construction drawings. I also want to illustrate the importance of having everyone agree on the design development submittal before the architect begins the working drawings. Redraws can be expensive. Do not take these hourly figures as anything but the broadest of numbers used for the sake of an example. Rates vary and the ever-present effects of inflation also have to be taken into account.

What the Architect Should Give You

The following is a brief description of a set of contract documents. Not every project has all the listed items, but the full list is helpful as a general outline.

☑ *Bidding requirements*

The bidding requirements are usually in five parts. They are usually on 8½ x 11 inch sheets and often are included as a part of the specification.

1. *Advertisement for Bids:* This document informs bidders of a project. It may be sent to selected contractors or to contractors who express interest in a project. See appendix C for an example.

2. *Instructions to Bidders:* This section incorporates by reference a standard AIA document, A701, and gives any modifications to be made to the standard document.

3. *Project Information:* This section gives general project information useful to bidders. It often takes the form of a project overview.

4. *Bid Form:* This is what contractors fill out to indicate the amount of their bids. They are sealed and returned to the library and usually opened at a public bid opening.

5. *Bid Bond:* This form guarantees that the contractor with the low bid will execute the contract at the agreed price within a specified length of time. If the contractor fails to do so, the library then accepts the next-lowest bid and the bonding company pays the library the difference, usually up to 10 percent of the amount of the first contractor's bid. If the agreement with the low bidder falls through, the 10 percent paid by the bonding company is intended to make up the difference between the lowest bid and the second-lowest bid. A special note: On rare occasions we have seen instances of contractors providing falsified bid bonds with nonexistent bonding companies. This is seldom a problem when dealing with reputable contractors, but it is wise to have your attorney verify the lowest bidder's bid bond.

☑ *Contract forms*

The contract forms usually include the following four sections:

1. *Agreement:* This is usually AIA document A101, the standard "Form of Agreement between Owner and Contractor," perhaps with modifications as suggested by the client's legal counsel.

2. *Performance Bond:* This bond guarantees that the contractor will perform the work agreed on. If the contractor fails to maintain the agreement, the bonding company must provide money to help the library get the work done by another contractor. Have your attorney confirm the validity of the performance bond, just as discussed relative to the bid bond, above. Performance and bid bonds are powerful tools. A bonding company does not issue bonds to contractors it feels are unable to complete the work or may be financially troubled. If a contractor's bond is called, it becomes

more difficult and expensive for that contractor to obtain future bonds. Bonds are significant incentives for contractors to complete their projects in accordance with the contract.

3. *Payment Bond:* This bond guarantees that the contractor will pay all retained subcontractors. If the contractor fails to do so, the bonding company provides money to pay the subcontractors to prevent them from placing liens on the client's property, in this case the library.

4. *Certificates:* This section includes various certificates the bidding documents require the contractor to furnish the client. Many of them are proof-of-insurance certificates.

☑ *Contract conditions*

The contract conditions are divided into two parts:

1. *General Conditions of the Contract:* This document is usually incorporated into the construction documents by reference. It is a standard AIA document that defines the parties to the contract and gives general information regarding the responsibilities of each. It covers many requirements, including the contractor's insurance requirements, resolution of disputes between client and contractor, how changes in the contract are to be handled, and how the contractor is to apply for payments. This is an important document. It defines your rights as the client and lists your responsibilities. It is important that the library board and its legal counsel have a basic understanding of this document's provisions.

2. *Supplementary Conditions to the Contract:* This document modifies the General Conditions of the contract to fit your particular circumstances. Because the General Conditions are stated in a preprinted, standard document, they cannot fit exactly the requirements of each project. Changes to the General Conditions are noted in this supplementary section. Public entities often have their own sets of requirements, some of which may contradict those in the General Conditions. The Supplementary Conditions document is where these special requirements are stated. The client's legal counsel often supplies many of these amendments. Other aspects of the Supplementary Conditions are discussed in chapter 9.

☑ *Specifications*

The specification is a document that sets the standards of quality for the construction, names products and materials that will be accepted, and itemizes additional responsibilities of the contractor. The specification is customarily divided into sixteen sections. The names of many of the sections are sufficient to describe their contents, but I add some examples where there could be some ambiguity. Each section contains many subsections, each covering a different product or system.

1. General Requirements. Sets forth general information relative to the specific project, usually administrative rules and work-related items such as office procedures, payment, and project meetings

2. Site Work

3. Concrete

4. Masonry

5. Metals

6. Wood and Plastics

7. Thermal and Moisture Protection. Includes insulation and caulk

8. Doors and Windows

9. Finishes

10. Specialties. Varied items including chalkboards, computer access floors, and toilet accessories

11. Equipment. Includes special library equipment and kitchen equipment

12. Furnishings. Movable furniture often specified and bid separately and not a part of the general building specifications

13. Special Construction. Includes atypical features such as special sound-controlled rooms, saunas, and whirlpools

14. Conveying Systems. Includes elevators and dumbwaiters

15. Mechanical. Ductwork, furnaces, chillers, and ventilation systems

16. Electrical

☑ *Drawings*

The drawings might consist of just several sheets for a small, interior remodeling project or run to a hundred sheets or more for a larger, new building. Drawings are divided into groups, the major ones being architectural drawings, structural drawings, mechanical drawings, plumbing drawings, and electrical drawings. Smaller, more specialized sections may be included for things such as kitchen equipment or specialties such as circulation desks and library equipment.

The drawings also contain schedules for items that are more appropriately presented in tabular format. These might include door types, room finishes, or hardware. Though it is difficult for the layperson to evaluate the completeness and accuracy of a set of drawings, it is relatively easy for the nonarchitect to look at some floor plans and get a basic understanding of what they represent. The future occupant can usually even find the answer to the most pressing question of all: How big is my office and does it have any windows? But things get a little more difficult when it comes to judging a wall section for its insulation value, or determining if a flashing detail will really keep the water out. That is the point when the client must rely on the expertise of the architect. The only real evaluations of the drawings can be done during the construction process, when you see if the project is proceeding smoothly, and after you move in, when you see how well the building really works.

What the Board Should Do

We have already touched on some of the client's duties during the construction documents phase. Here are some of the most important ones:

REVIEW THE DOCUMENTS. Review the documents with the architect several times during the construction documents phase. Keep current with the drawings as they evolve, for the architect will ask for your input at many points along the way. Selections of carpeting, toilet fixtures, door hardware, casework, and a hundred other items will need your approval. The architect will be showing you catalog illustrations of many of the items being proposed for your building along with relative costs. Allow the building committee to make decisions regarding smaller items and have the architect present the major ones to the full board for consideration.

GET A LAWYER INVOLVED. The board should have the library's legal counsel review all contract documents, especially the General Conditions and the client/contractor agreement, and suggest changes that seem to be in the best interest of the library. Any contract changes should be discussed and coordinated with the architect.

OBTAIN INSURANCE AND ACCOUNTING SERVICES. The client is responsible for providing insurance and accounting services as required to build the project. Your insurance agent and attorney can help with the appropriate amounts and types of insurance. Sometimes architects provide documents that already state minimum insurance requirements for the contractors. Often the information may be left over from previous projects. Never take the architect's word regarding what insurance is adequate for your project. Always have your insurance agent and attorney provide this information and transmit it to the architect for inclusion in the project documents.

ASK THE ENGINEER. Have your building engineer review designs and selections for the mechanical, electrical, and plumbing systems and verify that the systems selected are realistic and can be maintained by your staff. The maintenance staff should also be asked for their input on finishes and floor coverings they will be expected to maintain.

GET GOVERNMENT APPROVALS AND PERMITS. In the standard client/architect agreements, it is the responsibility of the client to submit the appropriate documents for the approval of the various government agencies that insist on having a say in your building project. Some of the permits are relatively obvious, like building permits, and some are less well-known. A few of the other agencies you might need to obtain permits from are the zoning board, the local sanitary district, the Environmental Protection Agency, the Army Corps of Engineers, and the state department of transportation. Others may be required, depending on your local and state requirements.

It may seem that you are wandering into a labyrinth of seemingly unrelated bureaucracies. Fortunately, your architect and the other consultants have found their way through this maze many times and can help you prepare and submit your documentation. Although the burden is on the client to file the documents, the architect and contractor customarily lend assistance. Ask your architect to put together a list of all the applicable permits, along with estimates of the time it will take for each government agency to process the paperwork. Keep this as a checklist for both the board and the architect and cover the subject of permits at each project meeting to track the process and ensure that none are overlooked.

Sign-Off

Once again, the board should formally accept the construction documents and sign off on a reference set retained by the library and another set the architect keeps. Dust off the project goals established during the programming phase and make a final review of the documents to verify that the project goals have been met. If some have not been met, it may be because of budget or other unavoidable limitations. Some of the goals may have changed during the course of the project. If you have been keeping good records, all changes in the project goals were noted as they were made. Good record keeping is important in charting the progress of your project.

A Bit of Advice: Reproducible Drawings

At the end of the construction document phase, the architect usually turns over several sets of drawings and specifications to the client. Usually these are in the form of prints made from the architect's original drawings. When forming your agreement with the architect, ask that the library be given reproducible copies of the drawings. Prints from the original drawings are reproducible only by the xerographic process. As they age, the prints tend to fade and yellow, which reduces the quality of subsequent prints that might be made from them. If the library has a reproducible set of drawings, it is always certain that additional sheets can be printed should they be needed for reference in the future. Ask that the prints be provided on a high-grade, acid-free paper.

If your project was produced on a computer-aided design (CAD) system, the drawings can be easily transferred to digital media and stored in the library's fire-proof records box. Note that you should still request hard copies, since electronic media have a limited useful lifespan. One of the best current options for long-term storage is the CD or DVD. Your architect can put the drawings on such media for a negligible cost.

Pay special attention to the format in which such documents are saved. Many clients ask for electronic copies in their original CAD format, the thought being that future architects will have easy access to the original drawings. Like most software, however, CAD programs are revised regularly. After several new versions, files from an earlier version of the program may no longer be readable by current versions. If you ask for electronic copies, discuss the options with the architect to ensure that you are getting a format that is likely to stand up to changes in the industry.

The reason for my concern about reproducible drawings is based on a personal experience. I was recently involved in a project at a community college, a large addition to an existing building. The existing building was only about twenty years old, but the college's set of working drawings had been lost. There's always someone who wants to borrow a set of building drawings—electricians might need to trace existing circuits, plumbers need to find valves, other architects doing remodeling work need the drawings to verify structural details. Unless an iron-willed building engineer takes responsibility for getting the drawings back, it is often just a matter of time before your set is incomplete or missing.

On this particular project, only a few of the sheets were still in the hands of the college. The architects who had done the original project had gone out of business several years earlier and consigned all their original drawings to a storage shed. Eventually these originals were discarded, along with any hope of ever determining exactly how the college's building was put together.

If you get a reproducible copy of your documents, keep them in a safe place away from the possibility of fire or water damage. You probably paid a good sum of money for these documents, so treat them as the investment they are. You must remember, however, that according to the standard client/architect contract, the original drawings and the design remain the property of the architect and cannot be reused without permission.

Chapter 8

Bidding

By the time a building project is bid, the architect and client have invested a large amount of time, energy, and money. When the drawings "hit the street" in search of bidders, the architect feels something like a parent whose child is going out into the world. The product you have slaved over, worried about, and nurtured is, for the first time, going to be exposed to the scrutiny and judgment of others. Like a new parent, we tend to have a lot of pride in what we have produced.

When contractors' calls and questions start coming in, the architect is brought suddenly back to earth and the work resumes. Sometimes the questions are tactfully presented. "Did you really mean to specify the gold-plated plumbing fixtures for the library director's washroom? It looks like it might be a typing error in the specification." At least this one leaves an easy way out. Sometimes the questions are honed to a slightly finer edge. "Are you sure that you want to put this kind of finish on the wood doors? You know what that'll look like in a few months, don't you?" Then there is the occasional, "How can you expect anybody to build this?" Every project needs its measure of clarifications and adjustments before it can be built. During the bidding phase, one of the architect's prime jobs is to iron out these rough spots and keep things running as smoothly as possible.

The culmination of the bidding process is, of course, the opening of the bids. That is the moment of truth, for all the cards are on the table. The desired outcome is a good number of consistent bids that fall comfortably within the project budget. Things are seldom so simple in real life, but with a little luck and some good planning, we can usually avoid scenarios like the one described for the fictional reroofing project in chapter 2. Even assuming good planning, the bids for a building project are influenced by numerous forces, many of them out of the control of the architect and client. Some of the variables are the local labor rates and the timing of the project with respect to the workload of the local contractors—in other words, the laws of supply and demand. The quality of the construction documents, unusual requirements requested by the client, and the time allotted for the construction of the project also influence the outcome of the bidding.

The mechanics of the bidding process should be understood by both the library representatives and the architect. For public work it is vitally important the standard procedures be followed and that everything conform to local and state regulations. Any irregularities could result in a legal challenge to your bids, potentially resulting in costly delays to your project. Be prepared to spend some time working with your architect and the library's legal counsel to guarantee that everything has been properly prepared. In many projects, the bidding phase usually represents approximately 5 percent of the architect's overall fee.

Project Options

Before we go into the particulars of the bidding process, let's take a look at a few of the different ways a project can be bid, and what they might mean to you. There are two basic ways a building project can be designed and bid. The most common method is by separate contracts for design and construction ("design-bid-build"); the second form utilizes a single contract for design and construction ("design-build"). Each method has advantages and drawbacks. This book is mainly based on the traditional design-bid-build method of project delivery. Design-bid-build is the most appropriate method of project delivery for most library projects. Sometimes, because of time constraints or other unusual circumstances, design-build or fast-track construction might be the right choice. See chapter 12 for comparisons of these different production methods.

Bidding Documents

We begin this section by assuming that the architect, working with the client, has produced a complete set of construction documents. Many of the documents involved, drawings and specifications, have been described in the previous chapters of this book. A portion of the construction documents is devoted to the conditions and requirements of the bidding process. Some of these documents are usually included as a portion of the specification. Let's look at several bidding documents and identify some things that should be included and some of the decisions the architect and client must make.

Advertisement for Bids

Most states require that, for public work, an advertisement for bids be published in a local or state newspaper and a building trade publication. Check with your legal counsel for the requirements in your area. Sometimes the advertisement must be placed in a publication with a specified minimum circulation and must run for a specified length of time. Refer to appendix C for a sample advertisement for bids that illustrates some of the information you should consider including.

Instructions to Bidders

The next part of the bidding documents is the Instructions to Bidders. This section incorporates by reference a standard AIA document, A701, and gives any modifications to be made to the standard document. Its purpose is to instruct the bidders on the general bidding requirements for a project and to define terms to help prevent ambiguity in the project documents. It states that each bidder, by submitting a bid, understands the bidding documents and has become familiar with local conditions as required to be a responsible bidder. Because some of the text refers to responsibilities of the client and to the client's financial capabilities, you should read the material in the instructions to bidders and make sure you understand the library's obligations.

Other sections of the instructions to bidders cover the interpretation of and corrections to the bidding documents, substitutions to items specified in the bidding documents, bidding procedures, and bond requirements. Discuss this section with your architect if you are unsure which sections are applicable to you, or if local regulations require changes to the standard form. Changes to the standard language are made in a separate section, the Supplementary Instructions to Bidders. Review this document to verify that it is consistent with your understanding of any changes you have discussed with the architect.

Bid Form

One or more copies of the bid form are usually distributed to each prospective bidder, and an additional copy is often included in the front of the specification. Bids are customarily presented in sealed envelopes. For public work they are usually opened at a public meeting and the bid amounts read aloud. The architect customarily prepares the bid form. As always, check with the library's attorney to verify that everything conforms to local regulations.

Client-Requested Alternates

When putting together the bid form, the client and architect may decide that it is advantageous to include one or more parts of the work as client-requested alternates. The purpose of alternates is often to ensure that the bids for the major part of the work fall within the project budget. Portions of the work that may push the project over budget, or that the board feels may cost more than they are worth to the library, are listed separately. The library board can decide later whether to include those parts of the work in the contract for construction. If properly selected, alternates help reduce the potential of all the bids coming in over budget, thus avoiding a potential rebid of the project. The cost breakdown alternates also give the board the chance to evaluate the costs of the selected portions of the work. As an example, let's assume the following:

1. The project construction budget is $3,000,000. This does not include a standing-seam metal roof for the main building or an outdoor story area for the children's library. For the "base bid," an asphalt shingle roof has been indicated and the story area has been omitted.

2. The architect's estimate for the building without the standing-seam metal roof or story area is $2,900,000. The metal roof has been designated Alternate #1 and the story area Alternate #2.

3. When the bids are received, the lowest bid for the base bid work (no metal roof or story area) is $2,850,000.

4. The low-cost bidder also bid $200,000 for inclusion of the metal roof.

5. That same low-cost bidder also bid $100,000 to include the story area.

We can immediately see the advantage of breaking those two items out of the base bid. If they had not been pulled out as separate items, the bid for the project would have been $3,150,000 ($2,850,000 + $200,000 + $100,000), which is over the project budget. If additional funds were not available, the only recourse would have been for the architect to redesign parts of the project and rebid it in the hope that it would come within the budget. This would be expensive for the library and could disrupt the construction schedule.

With the alternates, however, there is a recourse. The library could elect not to accept the alternate bids and proceed only with the base bid work. In this case, the contractor could be selected and hired, and the work could begin. The alternate bid for the metal roof would put the total cost at $3,050,000, which is over the project budget. The obvious question is, Couldn't we accept the base bid work and the second alternate bid and at least get the story area? This would give a total of $2,950,000, which is $50,000 under the limit. The answer is, Maybe not. For public libraries, some states require that the alternates be listed in order of preference and only accepted in that order. In this case, the cost of the metal roof put the project over budget, and you are not allowed to go on to the next alternate.

The rationale for this rule is that, by picking and choosing alternates, it would be possible to come up with a number of different "low bidders," depending on which alternates were selected. It would therefore be possible to steer the work to a favored contractor by juggling alternates. In most states, this kind of bid manipulation is illegal for public work. For private libraries, however, this rule often does not apply, and the client is free to select different combinations of alternates at will. For a large, complex project with lots of alternate bids, the process of selecting the low bidder can become very involved. In this case, the architect often prepares different combinations involving different alternates and presents them to the board for a decision. This process is called *bid analysis*.

Addenda

After the bidding documents are released to the public, the contractors begin to assemble their prices for the work. Costs are investigated and hours are estimated. During this period, many questions and requests for clarifications crop up, and the architect spends a lot of time on the phone responding to contractors' questions. To avoid any inequality in the bidding, any clarification or change that might result in a change to the bid amounts is issued to all the plan holders in the form of an addendum.

Addenda, when released, become a part of the bidding documents and carry the same authority as any of the drawings or specifications. There are sometimes legal limits on how close to bidding time addenda can be issued. Legalities aside, three days is often considered a practical minimum amount of time. A week would be better. General contractors may have to seek additional price information from suppliers for changes required by an addendum, and this process can take several days to accomplish.

Addenda are often issued in an 8½ x 11 inch format to allow them to be attached to the written project specifications as well as e-mailed to bidders who can then print the addenda themselves.

Bidding Process

Now that we've covered some of the bidding documents, let's look at an overview of the bidding procedure to see where these documents fit into the process. Listed below is the step-by-step procedure for bidding your project. These steps apply to most projects, although modifications may be required to suit your circumstances and conform with local regulations.

☑ Publish the advertisement

When the advertisement for bids and bid forms have been written, the process of bidding the project can begin. First the client publishes the advertisement for bids. The timing and placement of the publication are usually determined by state law. The advertisement is often required to be first published anywhere from two to five weeks before the date of the planned bid opening.

Contractors whom the library board is particularly interested in working with may be contacted directly and asked to submit a bid on the project. This is legal for a public library project as long as no contractor is given preferential treatment. An example of preferential treatment in this case would be giving the bidding documents to a desired bidder before they are generally available to other bidders.

☑ *Prequalify the bidders (optional)*

Contractors may be asked to prove that they are qualified and capable of doing the work described in the bidding documents. This can occur either before or after the bids are taken. Sometimes public bodies may have lists of "prequalified" contractors who have already been investigated and approved. The problem with this form of prequalification is that the lists often do not get updated. A contractor who may have been in fine financial shape when the list was drawn up could now be having difficulties that might jeopardize your project. The prequalification list might also have been assembled for a different kind of project than the one you are now undertaking. For example, a contractor deemed suitable for building a 2,000-square-foot addition might not be the appropriate choice for building a new library of 70,000 square feet. For these reasons, I recommend that prequalification be done on a project-by-project basis.

Sometimes contractors are required to become prequalified with the public body before they are allowed to obtain sets of bidding documents. This effectively limits the bidders to firms that have been prequalified and approved. An advantage to prequalification before bidding is that time is not wasted in evaluating bids that may later be disallowed because the contractor cannot meet the conditions of qualification. The disadvantage of prequalification is that much more time is spent up front in evaluating each firm that wants to bid on your project. If the architect is to do the prequalification screening, the time involved might not be included in the client/architect contract. If it isn't, the architect might be due additional fees.

In prequalifying bidders, there are several standard questions. The first thing to check is that the contractor has successfully built projects of comparable size and complexity. Second, the general financial condition of the contractor should be evaluated to determine if it can accommodate the cash flow requirement of a project your size. Quality of past work should also be considered. Speak to architects and clients who have worked with the contractor previously and get their opinions. This is a subjective measurement, however, and must be considered in that light. Finally, inquire about the bonding capacity of the contractor. If a surety company has investigated the contractor and approved the firm for bonding, it is an indication that the contractor is financially solvent.

The AIA has a standard form, Contractor's Qualification Statement (AIA Document A305), which is intended to help the client and architect screen contractors. It covers all the above material as well as additional items that assist evaluation of contractors. As with most other aspects of the bidding procedure, you should confirm the legality of prequalification with the library's legal counsel, since laws regulating bidding vary from state to state.

☑ *Hold a prebid conference*

Several weeks before the bids are due, a meeting should be arranged at the project site to enable potential bidders to ask questions regarding the project. If there is no suitable place at the project site, the meeting could take place in a conference room at the library. The architect attends, as should several members of the building committee. Careful minutes of the meeting should be kept and an attendance sheet passed around. The architect usually keeps the meeting minutes. Proof of attendance could be important in the event of a future dispute with a contractor regarding the work. Copies of the minutes should be distributed to all potential bidders and be included with any drawing sets that may subsequently be distributed. The date and location of the meeting should be included in the original bidding documents to ensure that all plan holders are duly informed of it. Any potential changes to the scope or content of the project documents should be noted in the meeting minutes. Any significant changes will be issued in the form of one or more addenda to the construction documents.

☑ *Issue addenda*

If changes are required in the project documents, the architect prepares addenda that itemize the modifications. These changes may result from the prebid meeting or from questions sent to the architect during the bidding period.

Because an addendum changes the scope of the work, there should always be a meeting between the architect and the building committee to ensure consensus on the form and content of the addendum before it is released to bidders. Since an addendum is in effect a contract document, the building committee should sign off on it before it is issued. Because of the time constraints of the bidding period, the building committee should be prepared to meet promptly to review addenda. Addenda should always be issued as far in advance of the bid opening as possible.

☑ *Open the bids*

When the date arrives for the opening of the bids, make certain that there is someone in the office to receive them as they are delivered. Check the accuracy of the library clock beforehand so you know when the deadline has passed. A measure like this might seem a bit overcautious but, considering the expense and effort that has to go into a rebid, it is worth spending a little extra effort up front.

At the appointed hour, a representative from the library should carry the bids to the room in which the opening is to take place and make an announcement that an open meeting has been called for the purpose of opening the bids. The official name of the project should be stated.

The sealed envelopes should be opened one at a time. The person reading the bids should publicly state the following:

- Name of the bidder
- Amount of the base bid
- Amounts of any alternate bids, in the order presented on the bid form
- Whether the bidder has acknowledged receipt of addenda
- Amount of the bid security enclosed with the bid
- General statement confirming that the bid appears to be in order (i.e., there are no additional notes and conditions attached to the bid form, or other irregularities)

When all the bids have been opened and read, the representative should thank any persons in attendance and close the public meeting. No interpretations of the bids should be offered, since the low bidder cannot be determined until the bids have been properly analyzed.

☑ *Analyze the bids*

Until the bids have been analyzed, the bidder with the lowest total bid is only the apparent low bidder. Alternates to the base bid must be examined and selected.

Each bid form must be thoroughly scrutinized to determine if it is acceptable. If the bidders were required to submit statements of qualification, the architect must first verify that the apparent low bidder is qualified according to the predetermined standards approved by the library board. The bid security is verified and, if it is in the form of a bond, the bonding company is investigated to ensure that its rating conforms with any requirements listed in the project documents. Bid security usually takes the form of a bid bond, as mentioned in chapter 7. A certified check for whatever amount is required for the bid bond is often acceptable. For public work, it is sometimes required that bids with any irregularities, such as additional notes attached by the contractor, be rejected.

If there are several bids, it is customary to return the bid securities promptly to all except the lowest three or four bidders. If the bid security is in the form of a certified check, unsuccessful bidders are understandably anxious to have them back. After a successful bidder has been selected and a contract signed, the remaining bid securities are usually returned.

☑ Sign the contract

When the successful bidder has been selected, the contract can be signed. The usual form is one of the AIA standard contracts, in this case AIA Document A101, Standard Form of Agreement between Owner and Contractor. Some government agencies and large corporations prefer to write their own client/contractor contract. Federal and state governments often have their own forms.

For the great majority of users, it makes sense to use the AIA contracts. Since the early 1900s, the AIA has been developing standardized contracts and forms. They have been developed with the benefit of years of experience and address most situations likely to come up during a construction project. The standard contracts are intended to reflect a consensus of organizations involved in the construction industry and attempt to remain unbiased toward any party. Considering the resources afforded by the standard documents, I recommend against asking your attorney to write a custom contract for an architectural project. It is not, however, unusual for a client's attorney to modify one of the standard contracts to satisfy the particular requirements of a project. This is almost always the option preferred to writing a custom contract.

Schedule a meeting with the chosen contractor, the architect, representatives of the building committee, and perhaps the library's attorney for the signing of the contract. Take this meeting as an opportunity to discuss the project with the contractor, who can use the occasion to bring up potential problems or opportunities from the construction point of view. The contractor often comes up with ideas for improving the project or expediting the work.

After the contract is signed, return the remaining bid securities to the unsuccessful bidders. As a courtesy, I usually enclose a brief note thanking them for their time and effort. Assembling a bid for a project of any magnitude is no small task, and a little recognition for their efforts is usually appreciated.

Birth of a Building

With a signed contract in hand, you are about to embark on an adventure. Nearly every day will bring a new challenge—some of them will be welcome opportunities, and others will require some difficult negotiations to sort out. Be prepared to devote a lot of your time and energy to the construction phase of your project. If you can keep the right attitude and regard the process as an adventure rather than a burden, you will find that you're able to relax more and enjoy it. It is not every day that you get the chance to attend the birth of a building!

Construction Administration

There's nothing like the start of a building project. The inevitable challenges encountered when making a building come together have yet to surface, and everything is still on schedule. It is an exciting time.

There is an untidy optimism as the contractor's forces are assembled on the site. Backhoes and earthmovers are marshaled in ragged lines. Piles of drain tile, concrete forms, rolls of fencing, and plastic sheeting are scattered in seeming disarray. Portable toilets appear, sometimes set on uneven ground and leaning at uncomfortable angles. In contrast to the apparent confusion, surveyor's stakes, in precise rows, neatly trace the outline of what will someday be a library.

A Commercial Break

One of the most memorable events of the long process of building a new library, or of adding an addition, is the groundbreaking. The ceremonial first shovelfuls of earth are dug, cameras click, flashes flash, maybe a speech is made, and then the party breaks up. The local newspaper might have photographs of a smiling group, each person holding a gold shovel. The casual newspaper reader, pausing at the photograph, usually has little idea of the amount of time and effort the team has expended to get the project this far. The team members themselves may underestimate the amount of time and effort that it's going to take to finish this trip. Much remains to be done, many lessons to be learned, and many decisions to be made before the keys to a new building are handed over.

Being a memorable event, the groundbreaking should be milked for all its inherent publicity value. Good public relations are important for any tax-supported institution, and we should always look for opportunities to increase public involvement in the library. The construction phase offers some good opportunities for media exposure. Some frequent library users could be invited to participate in the groundbreaking. Get your state senator or representative to lay the first brick. Cornerstones with time capsules offer a golden opportunity to stimulate public interest. Contests might be held at different levels of the local schools to select the contents of the capsule. See if the local Kiwanis Club will donate and plant the first tree when it's time to put in the landscaping. If there's a local garden club, see if the members will take over the design and maintenance of one or two of the flower beds. Wring it out for all it's worth and insist that the local newspaper cover everything. If your funding comes from referenda and property levies, you owe it to the taxpayers to show them what their money is buying and to give them a feeling of involvement with their new library.

A Changing Project Team

During the construction phase of the project, the composition of your project team changes and the players' responsibilities are somewhat altered. The involvement of the library staff diminishes as the design they helped shape moves into the

The beginnings and endings of all human undertakings are untidy, the building of a house, the writing of a novel, the demolition of a bridge, and, eminently, the finish of a voyage.

—John Galsworthy

Things are always at their best in the beginning.

—Blaise Pascal

construction phase. The library director and building engineer should continue to offer their input during the construction phase, for many questions will come up that they are best qualified to answer.

During this time the architect also takes on new responsibilities in order to get your building built. We looked at the nature of the architect/client relationship back in chapter 2. The agency relationship, in which the architect is empowered to act on behalf of the client, is most pronounced during the construction phase. The architect will be making many decisions that are binding on you, the client. Contractor's pay requests are authorized, judgments are rendered on the acceptability of the contractors' work, meetings are scheduled and shop drawings reviewed. For the architect, construction contract administration is a time-consuming task. In a typical project, it accounts for about 20 percent of the architect's fee.

Remember also that the architect may be required to act as an impartial arbiter in the event of disputes between client and contractor. That is where the nature of the services offered by the architect is a little different from that of many other professionals. You pay an attorney to remain strictly "on your side" no matter what. Your case might be groundless and your judgment faulty, but you know that your lawyer is going to back you up. You pay an architect, on the other hand, not only to represent you but also to get a building built. On certain occasions during construction, those two functions can come into conflict. This is especially true in the case of disagreements between clients and contractors. On those occasions, the architect is required by the construction contract to render an impartial decision consistent with the terms of the contract. While somewhat unusual, this concept is time-tested and has been shown to be an effective way to get your building built.

This role seldom results in an adversarial relationship between client and architect. In the final analysis, the client controls the purse strings and has final say on the disbursement of funds. If you found yourself in some irreconcilable disagreement with your architect regarding a conflict with a contractor, it would be possible to terminate the architect's contract, pay for the architect's services to date, and to try to find a different architect who would see things your way. Meanwhile, there is a new character who might be involved in your project and who is always in your corner: the owner's representative.

Owner's Representative

For an institution that is controlled by a board of trustees, like many libraries, it can be difficult to assemble the group each time a quick decision is required. In addition, the library director usually has enough to do without having to give constant attention to the building project. In this case, the board might decide to retain an "owner's representative," sometimes referred to as the "clerk of the works." The owner's representative represents and acts on behalf of the client at the job site. This person can relieve the library director and board of many of the mundane, day-to-day tasks that must be addressed while the building is being built and take over many of the routine interactions with the architect and contractor. A representative experienced in the construction of buildings and with the right personality is a valuable asset to any project.

Great care should be exercised in selecting an owner's representative. Giving the task to the wrong individual can have serious repercussions and disrupt the delicate balance of the relationships among the client, contractor, and architect. I advise that you look for an individual who stresses cooperation rather than a "junkyard dog" who guarantees to settle every dispute to the library's advantage. Some of the primary qualifications are a thorough knowledge of construction and an even disposition. Some retired contractors or architects make good representatives.

Ask other institutions in your area that have built recently if they utilized an owner's representative. Your state library may also be able to steer you toward qualified individuals. The owner's representative is a strictly optional position. Discuss the concept with the library director and board to see if there is a consensus on whether an owner's representative would help your project.

I know of some clients who feel they need an owner's representative "to keep an eye on the architect." That is always an option if you think your architect is less than trustworthy. When I hear this rationale, I always respond by asking who the client is hiring to keep an eye on the client's attorney, financial advisor, or dentist. And then, come to think of it, why did they hire an architect they don't trust?

Some hopeful owner's representatives try to convince clients of the need for their services by implying that they are required to protect the project from "scope-creep," when architects allow the size or scope of a project to increase either innocently or with the intention of generating increased fees for themselves. In reality, architects are like everyone else associated with the project; they have to live within the established budget. If there is still some lingering uncertainty, a few calls to prospective architects' previous clients should be sufficient to confirm that they understand the importance of budget control. The standard AIA Owner/Architect contract (B141) states that the architect may be liable for a redraw if the project comes in over the agreed budget. This provides a powerful incentive for the architect to monitor cost control.

If you decide to hire an owner's representative, the board should first decide exactly how much authority should be vested in this individual. The job description should be worked out in detail to reduce the potential for confusion later. Your architect might be able to assist you in identifying potential assignments and in determining the scope of the owner's representative's responsibilities. See appendix F for a proposed list of responsibilities you might want to assign to an owner's representative.

One last thought about hiring an owner's representative: some owner's representatives want to be included in the selection process for the architects. I recommend against this because the owner's representative may have preexisting relationships with architects from other projects; such dealings with potential architects could influence the selection process, which should remain the responsibility of the library board.

Chain of Command

The library board should establish a chain of command for dealing with changes, adjustments, and minor emergencies during the construction phase, just as in the design phase. Items that involve a significant adjustment to construction costs or the estimated completion date should always be brought before the board for discussion and approval. Other individuals involved in the project should be empowered to make decisions about items that do not affect the contract. You should decide who is empowered to make the decisions and define the limits of their responsibility. The typical chain of responsibility for problem resolution would start with the owner's representative (if you have one), move up to the library director, then to the building committee, and end with the full board of directors.

Just how far a particular type of problem should move up this ladder of responsibility should be defined at the start of the project. The architect is, of course, available at all points of this process to lend assistance.

Project Representative

In addition to, or as an alternate to, employing an owner's representative, the architect can supply a project representative. This should be considered for fast-track jobs and other projects of particular complexity. A full-time project representative is not included in the standard Owner/Architect contract and is usually billed as an additional service. A project representative performs many of the same services the architect provides but gives the advantage of a quick turnaround time and nearly continuous job site observation.

It is important that the client realize that the standard Owner/Architect contract does not make the architect responsible for continual or exhaustive on-site observation. If you feel that your project calls for this kind of attention, discuss the options with your architect. In most cases, architects make job site visits once every week or two unless you opt for additional on-site representation.

Construction

I always look forward to hearing individual reactions to a new building when it begins to take shape. "It's so much (bigger, smaller, taller, shorter, brighter, dimmer, harder, softer, more impressive, more understated, better, worse, redder, bluer, greener . . .) than I thought it was going to be." The average person is not accustomed to reading plans, and the finished product is usually something of a revelation. This also happens to the architect. We usually have a better idea just what the building is going to look like, but there are always surprises—some of them pleasant. We may never have realized how good a job we did integrating the building into the neighborhood context, and while patting ourselves on the back we notice that something like the rooftop mechanical units are a lot more prominent than we ever intended.

Every job has its share of surprises. With a little study, you can acquaint yourself with the general game plan of a construction project. This won't eliminate the unexpected, but it might make you better prepared to deal with it when it comes.

Early in this book I spoke of the need for a common language between architect and client. Think of this chapter as a kind of grammar lesson where we learn some of the rules by which buildings are built. The aim is give you the same understanding as your architect of some of the more important concepts. Every project is different, but much of what follows should apply to your situation.

Preconstruction Meeting

When a contract for construction has been awarded, one of the first orders of business is to hold a meeting to set the ground rules for the project. With a little effort, this meeting can set a precedent for effective communication among all the players during construction. The architect usually prepares the agenda for and runs this preconstruction meeting, covering these major items:

☑ *Introductions*

Everyone who will be involved in project management should be introduced and have their responsibilities detailed. The architect or contractor should prepare a project directory that gives the names and phone numbers of each individual with management responsibilities. Identify the people who should be contacted in case of emergency.

☑ *Notice to proceed*

The contractor should be given a formal, signed notice to proceed. This is issued and signed by the client. The notice establishes the official date of the beginning of construction. The General Conditions state that the contractor may begin work on receipt of the notice. If a set amount of time has been set by contract for the construction of the building, the clock begins ticking with the contractor's receipt of the notice to proceed.

☑ *General and Supplementary Conditions of the contract*

During the preconstruction meeting, the architect should review the General and Supplementary Conditions of the project documents with the contractor and owner's representative. These documents contain information that will govern much of the day-to-day administration of the construction project. They also define the responsibilities of the client and contractor. Some of the items on this checklist are drawn from provisions in the General and Supplementary Conditions.

☑ *Schedule and provisions for payments to the contractor*

The procedure and timing for payments to the contractor should be discussed. Before each payout, there are specific things the contractor must provide and the client and architect must do. These are defined in the General Conditions of the contract. All parties should review the requirements to ensure that everyone understands the procedures. At each pay request, the architect will certify that the contractor has completed all the work billed. The timing of requests for payment should be worked out to dovetail with board meetings, where the contractor's payments are approved. Usually, request for payment should be required a week to ten days before board meetings to give the architect sufficient time to review and comment on pay requests.

☑ *Project schedule*

A project schedule should be established and milestone dates set for significant construction events. These dates are helpful for following the progress of the work. Keep in mind that, no matter how pressing your project schedule, many things can disrupt the most carefully laid plans. Many of them are out of the control of the contractor, such as bad weather, labor strikes, and unforeseen site conditions.

☑ *Project meetings*

A schedule and format for project meetings should be established, along with a minimum agenda. Meetings may be held only at payouts or more frequently, depending on circumstances. The person responsible for keeping and distributing meeting minutes should be named, as should the representatives who are to attend the meetings.

☑ *Miscellaneous*

Before the preconstruction meeting, the building committee should meet and make a list of items of special concern to the library. The list could form part of the agenda for the preconstruction meeting. Items on this list might include the contractor's access to the site, the use of library washrooms and phones by the contractor's personnel, parking, and site cleanup. Many of these items are also covered in the General Conditions to the contract. Contractors' personnel have varying degrees of familiarity with the General Conditions; it never hurts to review the ones that are particularly important to you.

Field Reports

Lines of communication established during the preconstruction meeting must be kept open throughout the course of the project. For the client, it can be difficult to keep up with the work at the construction site. To keep you informed, the architect periodically assembles written summaries of the work. These summaries, called *field reports,* are a useful tool for keeping you abreast of the progress of the project.

At the start of construction the architect should begin supplying you with field reports, written by the architect's field representative. The field report need not be lengthy, but it should cover all important information relevant to the project. Items that might be included are the progress of the work to date, notes on the acceptability of work completed, actual task completion relative to the proposed schedule, and detailed information regarding particular portions of the work (e.g., structural steel, masonry, door hardware).

New and potential problems should also be identified. The timing of the field reports should parallel the pace of the work. During periods of intense activity, the architect or architect's field representative may write biweekly or even daily field reports. The owner's representative or the building committee should review all field reports.

Change Orders

Change orders are a normal, if often unwelcome, part of the construction process. With the many uncertainties inherent in a building project, it is inevitable that adjustments will have to be made en route to cope with the unexpected. They can be a source of tension within the construction team.

During construction, thousands of decisions are made by the contractor, the architect, and the client. Many of these are made to resolve items not completely covered in the contract documents. When one of these decisions results in a measurable change in the contract price, the time required to complete the contract, or the scope of the final product, a change order should be prepared to document the changes in the construction contract formally.

Architects commonly use Document G701, the standard AIA form for change orders. This standard form covers all of the above information and is designed to be convenient and easy to understand. With change orders possessing so much potential for misunderstanding and conflict, it is important that we look at the architect's and client's roles in the change order process. Change orders should include at least the following information:

- Name and address of the project.
- Number and date of the change order.
- Written description of the change, referencing drawings and other appropriate backup material as required.
- Amount of the change order and any changes to the project schedule.
- New contract price.
- Signatures of the client, contractor, and architect. The signatures attest that each has reviewed the contents of the change order and agrees to the conditions of the document.

ARCHITECT'S RESPONSIBILITIES REGARDING CHANGE ORDERS

The architect is responsible for writing change orders, typically filling in all the information on the change order form except the new price, which the contractor adds. After the contractor signs and returns the change order to the architect, the architect evaluates the price and, if no exception is taken, signs the document and forwards it to the client. If so directed, the architect should be prepared to come before the board or the building committee to explain the reasons for and scope of the change.

All change orders are issued in the client's name and are contingent on the approval of the client. The architect does not have the authority to approve any changes to the construction contract without the written approval of the client.

CLIENT'S RESPONSIBILITIES REGARDING CHANGE ORDERS

The change order process is a way for a client to make changes to a previously signed contract without invalidating it. Because they represent changes in the construction contract, change orders should come before the building committee or entire board. For public agencies, the proposed changes should be reviewed and approved in an open meeting. If so directed, the architect presents a description of the proposed changes to the board along with an analysis of the cost of and rationale for the changes.

If the client requests the change order, it is the client's responsibility to keep the work defined by the change order within the general range of the scope of work covered in the original contract. A contract for a 2,000-square-foot addition to a library cannot be transformed by change order into a contract for a new library of 20,000 square feet. Changes must also not be of such a nature as to render the selected contractor incapable of performing the work.

Ask the library's attorney if your state has any regulations controlling the extent of change orders. Some states limit the size of change orders in publicly funded work to a fixed percentage of the project cost so that changes in the contract cannot be used as a vehicle for circumventing public bidding laws.

In addition to the potential additional cost of construction stated in a change order, the client may owe the architect additional professional fees. Architect's fees are often set as a percentage of the cost of the completed project. If this is the case, then the increase in professional fees is applied automatically when the final cost of the project is tallied. If the architect's contracted fee was a lump sum arrangement based on the scope of work, then the architect is justified in negotiating an increase in the fee to cover the additional time spent on the change order documentation.

Things can, of course, work the other way around. If a change order is needed because of a mistake on the part of the architect or contractor, the cost of the change order might be borne by someone other than the client.

WHO PAYS?

For a two-word question, this one certainly packs a lot of punch. Some people seem more concerned with who is footing the bill than with what is being purchased. Regarding change orders, sometimes the answer to this question is straightforward, and many times it's not. The responsibility for payment of each change order must always be considered in light of the particular circumstances that resulted in the need for the change. Depending on those circumstances, the client, the contractor, a supplier, or the architect might be responsible for bearing the cost of a change order.

Although they are always issued in the name of the client, change orders can be requested by either the client, the contractor, or the architect. Let's look at several possible scenarios that might result in the issuance of a change order, as well as at who might be responsible for footing the bill for the work.

STRAIGHTFORWARD. During the construction project, the library director approaches the library board with a request to change the finish on the walls of his office from painted drywall to walnut paneling. "All the other library directors get walnut paneling in their offices," he says. Moved by the persuasive power of his argument, the board immediately agrees to his request. You, as the chair of the building committee, direct the architect to begin a change order. In this case it's simple. The architect prepares the change order, draws a few new details, and gives it to the contractor for pricing. The additional cost is added to the contract and is borne by the library. Whether by percentage fee or negotiation, the architect's fee is increased to cover the costs of time. This is what is commonly referred to as a *client-requested* or *value-added* change order.

STILL STRAIGHTFORWARD. Your architect reports that a basement sump pump was somehow omitted from the drawings. "Not to worry," she says. "We caught the mistake in plenty of time. Just sign this change order, and we'll have the contractor order the pump." According to the change order form, the new pump will cost $2,000. Who is going to pay for it? In a case like this, the pump should have been included in the drawings in the first place and was left off by the architect. Still, it is something the library would have had to pay for anyway. In these cases, the additional cost often comes out of the money set aside for project contingency funds and the work moves on. This kind of change order is considered to be the result of an omission by the architect. When an item is added to a contract at this point of the project, it usually costs somewhat more than if it had been included in the drawings and competitively bid. Sometimes the architect's percentage-based fee does not include the value of omission change orders. This helps make up for any cost increase caused by the lack of competitive bidding. Additionally, the cost of any new drawings, specifications, or other tasks related to the pump might be borne by the architect.

NOT SO STRAIGHTFORWARD. An hour later your architect reports, "I was wrong about catching the mistake in plenty of time. They poured that part of the basement slab yesterday, and we'll have to tear up some of it to install the pump. The contractor says that it's going to cost an extra $5,000 to tear up and replace the concrete."

You could understand paying the $2,000 for the pump since you needed it anyway, but the additional $5,000 seems a different matter. The architect has done a lot for the library. She donated a lot of her time during the referendum, making speeches and generally helping to get your message out to the voters. What do you do? Could the additional money also come out of the project contingency or is the library required to try to get it out of the architect? What are your choices?

A FINE MESS . . . You're spending some time working out your options, trying to figure out who is going to pay for the change order, when the architect rushes into your office. "We need a stop-work order right away! I was out there watching them tear up the slab when I noticed that it was a four-inch slab, not the six-inch one shown on the drawings—the contractor should be the one paying for the replacement of the slab, not me!" Things seem to be looking up for her, and you call in the contractor to discuss the matter. The architect opens up the set of drawings, "See, here on sheet A3, the foundation detail clearly shows the slab as being six inches thick." The contractor opens up his set of drawings and flips through one dog-eared sheet after another. "Yes, but . . . ," he begins, "The structural details on sheets S1 and S2 show the slab as four inches thick. One place you say six inches, another place you say four inches. Which one am I supposed to believe? It looks like it's your mistake after all. And on top of that, the backhoe we brought in to tear up your slab backed into a delivery truck and smashed a load of walnut paneling. Who pays for that?"

You decide that maybe it's time to schedule a special meeting of the building committee to try to iron things out. The architect and contractor promise to attend the meeting and, in the meantime, the project will proceed. As the Porsche and the pickup leave the parking lot, you call the personnel manager to check on how much vacation time you still have coming for the year.

◇   ◇   ◇

We are not going to try to untangle the entire mess. It is just intended to illustrate how difficult it can be to stay on top of things. The General Conditions of the contract usually state that the contractor is responsible for thoroughly reviewing the contract documents, noting any discrepancies and bringing them to the attention of the architect for resolution; that's why you have the prebid and the preconstruction meetings. But it's not necessarily that simple. Resolving situations like this takes a careful study of the contracts as well as a close look at the relevant circumstances.

One aspect of the above scenario should be examined. When it was discovered that the concrete slab had been poured and had to be removed in order to place the sump pump, the change order assumed a different identity—actually a dual identity. You always needed the sump pump; no one disputes that. You pay for the pump from the project contingency funds and the architect may or may not receive a fee for that portion of the work. The replacement of the concrete slab is a different matter; that represents costs for which you should not have to pay. This portion of the change order becomes a Change Order due to Error. In this case, the architect or contractor may have to foot the bill for this work. Straightening out which of them is responsible for this cost remains to be resolved. You can imagine that this kind of situation can be responsible for disputes among the various players, with everyone looking for someone else to blame.

The architect's or contractor's liability for change orders due to error is usually limited to the amount of actual damages experienced by the client. Adding a sump pump that was omitted in the drawings might increase the cost of the building by several thousand dollars, but the client is getting added value and shouldn't expect someone else to pay for it; there are no damages involved in that scenario. Having to pay the contractor to tear out and repour a new concrete slab in order to install the pump represents potential damages. In this case, the architect may have to bear the cost of the concrete work.

DEAL WITH IT AND MOVE ON

In your role as chair of the building committee, you might have been a little confused about how such a matter should be settled, but you certainly did at least one thing right: you brought it to the table right away and scheduled the special board meeting to work out the issue. It can be tempting to put matters like this aside and delay making decisions until the end of the job, when things will be a little less hectic. In practice, that's usually not a good idea. As often as not, the architect and contractor end the project making less profit than they had planned during those optimistic times when the construction was just beginning. They may be in no mood to bargain when it's time for the final reckoning. In addition, closing out a project is enough of a task without adding a whole series of negotiations involving mistakes that may have been made a year or more ago. When preparing to issue a change order, always try first to settle the question of who is going to be financially responsible for it.

The seeming inevitability of changes in the work illustrates the importance of the construction contingency fund. Usually around 5 percent of the estimated cost of the project, this money is held back to cover eventualities like the walnut paneling and sump pump. Refer to chapter 6 for additional discussion on contingency.

Shop Drawings

As the construction project begins, the contractor is placing orders for many pre-manufactured and custom-built items to be installed in the building. As a way of ensuring that they have understood the project documents, the manufacturers first prepare detailed drawings of items they propose to supply to the contractor. These *shop drawings* are customarily reviewed first by the contractor, then by the architect. On approval by both parties, the drawings are sent back to the manufacturer, who then fabricates the items. On occasion the architect consults you regarding the acceptability of a shop drawing. For the most part, however, this process is not apparent to the client—most of the review and acceptance of the drawings being undertaken by the architect and contractor.

According to the standard AIA General Conditions, the architect reviews shop drawings only to verify that they conform to the general intent of the construction documents. The architect's approval of the drawings does not relieve the contractor of the responsibility of providing what is called for in the specifications and construction drawings. This may seem like something of a cover-your-behind move on the part of architects, but there are sound reasons behind it. Architects are understandably reluctant to assume responsibility for someone else's drawings. As an example, some shop drawings arrive at the architect's office looking as if they had been sent over directly from NASA—impeccably drafted, perfectly dimensioned, and with copious notes to the person who eventually fabricates the item. Other shop drawings seem like afterthoughts drawn on the back of a napkin at a truck stop. On top of it all, the quality of shop drawings is not a certain guide to the caliber of the finished product.

The bottom line is that the sophistication of shop drawings varies greatly. Regardless of any reviews and approvals by the architect, the contractor is ultimately responsible for providing the client with the building described in the contract documents.

Progress Payments

The architect, as the agent of the client, is responsible for monitoring the progress of construction and processing the contractor's pay requests. Each pay request is evaluated by the architect before it is submitted to the client. The architect takes several things into account in evaluating a request for payment. Several of the more important ones are listed below.

SCHEDULE OF VALUES. At the beginning of the construction phase, the contractor should provide the architect and the client with a schedule of values. The schedule of values assigns monetary values to the various general categories of work. The work is broken down into parts, such as foundations, excavation, structural steel, and masonry, and a value for each portion of the work is given. These amounts, added to the contractor's profit and overhead, add up to the total amount of the contractor's bid. Contractors are typically paid only for work completed as of the date of the pay request. Because the schedule of values defines the worth of parts of the project, it is a valuable tool for the architect (and the client) for comparing the contractor's requests for payment against the amount of work completed to date. For example, if a contractor has declared that the foundation work is worth $300,000 on the schedule of values and his first pay request asks for $200,000 for foundations, it should be a relatively easy matter for the architect to verify that approximately two-thirds of the foundation work has indeed been completed.

APPLICATION FOR PAYOUT. The timing of the payments to the contractor was previously established in the General Conditions and should have been discussed at the preconstruction meeting. As these dates draw near, the contractor sends an application for payment to the architect. This application may be in the form of standard ALA documents, or it may be the contractor's own standard forms.

On receipt of the application, the architect first verifies that the contractor has completed the work being billed and then compares the amounts against the schedule of values. In addition to verifying the amount of completed work, the architect also checks that the contractor has paid the subcontractors and suppliers. This is an important detail, since it can protect the library from legal complications.

LIEN WAIVERS. The lien waiver is the architect's prime tool for ensuring that the contractor has paid any project-related debts owed to subcontractors and suppliers. The waiver itself is a preprinted form the subcontractor or supplier completes. The form states which project the subcontractor is working on, for whom, and how much the contractor has paid the subcontractor to date.

If a contractor retained by the library defaults on payments to subcontractors or suppliers who have provided goods and services for the construction of your project, they could file liens against your property. Often called *mechanic's liens,* these instruments are attached to the title of the library's property and can prevent any transfer of the title until the payments are honored. In some jurisdictions they can be foreclosed like an unpaid mortgage. The threat posed to your library by liens varies from one state to another. In some states, contractors cannot file a lien against any public entity. In any event, the architect attempts to verify that the contractor has paid the subcontractors and suppliers before any payments to the contractor are approved.

CERTIFYING THE PAYMENT. After the waivers are checked and the amount of the request for payment is approved, the architect processes the pay request by issuing a certificate for payment. This completed form is forwarded to the client, often with copies of lien waivers. Receipt of a certified pay request indicates that the architect has evaluated the pay request and considers the contractor to be due the payment.

PAYMENT. As a part of the standard AIA General Conditions you, as the client, are contractually required to make payments to the contractor in the amounts certified by the architect within a specified time frame. This protects the contractor from a client who might wish to withhold a payment arbitrarily even if the work has been provided per the contract requirements. The General Conditions also require the contractor to adhere to the architect's decisions regarding payment. If the architect determines that the contractor is due less money than was requested on the pay request, the contractor is equally bound by the architect's decision. This is another one of the occasions where the architect assumes the role of impartial arbiter of the construction contract.

Retainage

When a client makes a payment to a contractor, a portion of the total amount due—usually 5–10 percent, is customarily retained by the client until the final completion of the project. In many states, retainage is required for public work. Retainage is held by the client to ensure that the contractor completes all the work contracted. At the end of each project, even after the client has taken occupancy, there are hundreds of small items that need to be completed, adjusted, or replaced by contractors and their subcontractors. If a contractor has completed and been paid for 99.5 percent of the work, it might not be worth that contractor's time to send workers to the library to take care of that last half percent. The 5–10 percent held back by the client might be roughly equivalent to the contractor's profit on the entire project. Thus, it is a significant incentive for the contractor to complete the project fully. If a retainage is going to be withheld, the architect accounts for it on the certificates for payment.

Retainage is often released to the contractor as a part of the final payment. Alternately, retainage may be partially or fully released to the contractor at some point during the project. The General and Supplementary Conditions of the contract contain information regarding the disposition of the retainage. There are three items to consider if an early release of retainage is being considered. One is that you will be giving up some of the leverage you possess to force the contractor to complete the project. Second, if your library is a public library, the library's attorney must verify that your state's laws permit an early release of the money. Finally, if a performance bond was required as a part of the General Conditions, the contractor's bonding company must preapprove the release of the retainage.

Punch List

At some point, the new building is declared ready to occupy. Don't confuse being ready to occupy with being complete, for there will surely be many small items that require the contractor's attention. When the building is sufficiently complete for the client to take possession, the contractor asks the architect to do a walk-through and record all the items that haven't been completed or are otherwise unacceptable. This record is called the *punch list* (see appendix D for an example).

The library director or another representative of the client should accompany the architect on the walk-though. Have the library staff prepare a list of their own and submit that list to the architect (not the contractor) before the formal walk-through. Extra sets of eyes never hurt.

All sorts of things can appear on a punch list—ideally none of them will be major items, for the building is supposedly ready to occupy. Entries might include things like a door frame that didn't get painted, a bad seam in the carpeting, a dripping faucet, finger marks on a ceiling tile, or a squeaking belt in a ventilating unit. Don't be shy about pointing out things that do not meet with your approval. This is your chance to make sure that every detail is complete and that the taxpayers have gotten their money's worth.

A thoroughly prepared punch list is doubly important after the building is occupied, for the contractor could claim that any defects that don't appear on the list were caused by the library staff or patrons, and thus are not the contractor's responsibility.

Substantial Completion

When the walk-through is complete and the punch list has been written, the architect declares the project "substantially complete" and issues a *certificate of substantial completion,* which states that the building is sufficiently complete for the client to occupy it for its intended use. Note that there may still be outstanding items on the punch list at the time of substantial completion. The architect, client, and contractor must all sign the certificate to indicate their acceptance.

The certificate of substantial completion has several important implications for you, as the client. It is important that you understand them:

1. The date on which the building is declared to be substantially complete is the moment when the clock begins running on all the guarantees and warranties the contractor provides you. The entire building is usually covered by a one-year guarantee, and many of the items within the building may be covered with more extensive warranties of their own. Wood doors might have a two-year warranty against warping, and blower motors in the air conditioning system might have a three-year warranty against mechanical failure. These periods of coverage begin at substantial completion. Insofar as guarantees are concerned, it would benefit the library to delay the date of substantial completion as long as possible.

2. On substantial completion, much of the retainage is usually returned to the contractor. If there are many items remaining on the punch list, the library is thus losing some of its bargaining power with the contractor to get these items taken care of. It is also losing the use of the retainage funds. In addition, punch list items still outstanding at substantial completion almost invariably mean headaches later. If your schedule can support a delay, it might be worth your while to delay the substantial completion until most of the items on the punch list have been completed.

3. On substantial completion, the client assumes responsibility for providing insurance and utilities as well as building security. Any damage to the building that occurs after this date is at the client's expense. Have your office manager verify that the library's insurance is in order before signing a substantial completion document.

4. So far, we have seen three good reasons to delay the date of substantial completion. On the other hand, you cannot take possession of the building until substantial completion has been declared. If you are on a tight schedule, it may even be necessary to move up the date of substantial completion and move into the building with more items on the punch list than you would prefer. In this case, you might ask the architect if it is possible to hold onto a larger portion of the retainage to cover for the amount of work that remains.

Because much of the responsibility for the building is transferred from the contractor to the client at substantial completion, the contractor is usually anxious to have as early a date of substantial completion as possible. Knowing some of the other factors involved, you should now be better prepared to try to time this event to the best advantage of the library.

Certificate of Occupancy

One of the last formalities prior to moving into your new building is obtaining a *certificate of occupancy* from your local building officials. Depending on where you are building, it may also be necessary to get the blessing of the state fire marshal and elevator inspector, among others. The local building officials have most likely been regular visitors to the construction site. They often are required to grant approvals for many parts of a building. Foundations, framing, electrical, and plumbing systems typically are inspected as the building is being constructed. The contractor is usually responsible for calling the authorities and scheduling the inspections for the appropriate times.

If all is going well, you might not be aware of their visits. If the inspectors find some major flaw or code violations, you'll be among the first to know. Assuming that your building has passed all the interim inspections, you are ready to obtain the certificate of occupancy. The responsibility for obtaining this certificate, as well as others that may be required during construction, is usually assigned in the General Conditions of the contract. This is a good time to review this document to satisfy yourself that you and the other players are all fulfilling your contractual duties.

Final Completion

While you are moving in and preparing to open, the contractor's crews have been busy completing the punch list items. Many items may still need to be addressed after you have opened the doors to the public. Eventually the contractor will declare that all the items on the punch list have been completed, send the architect a written notice of completion, and request a last inspection and final payment.

According to the General Conditions, the architect should promptly schedule a final walk-through to verify that all punch list items have been completed to the architect's and client's satisfaction. A representative of the client should again accompany the architect on the final inspection. While making the inspection, do not forget that the contractor is primarily responsible only for items listed on the punch list. There are some exceptions, but the onus rests with the architect and client to prove that any additional unacceptable conditions did not arise since the date of substantial completion.

After determining that all outstanding items have been completed, the architect issues a statement of final completion to the client. This defines the formal end of the contract time. The architect also begins to process the contractor's final payment application. As with the other applications for payment, the architect requires the contractor to supply lien waivers from all the general contractor's subcontractors and suppliers. In this instance, all the lien waivers are "final waivers of lien." A final waiver signifies that the general contractor has completed the contracts with the subcontractors and suppliers and made final payment to them.

Before final payment can be made to the contractor, the contractor's surety company must be notified and its permission obtained. The standard AIA Consent of Surety Form, signed by an authorized representative of the company, must be submitted by the contractor. Obtaining the surety company's approval and verifying the final waivers helps prevent challenges to the library's property. The importance of these measures cannot be overstated, especially with public property. Have the library's attorney check over and approve all the final closeout documents before signing them. When the final payment is made to the contractor, the title for the property formally passes to the client. Under the General Conditions, the contractor warrants that the property is clear of liens and other claims.

> ### BEFORE THE OPENING
>
> If you have a deadline for occupying the new building, it might make sense to have the architect contact the local building authorities in advance to verify that they expect to issue the certificate of occupancy. Nothing puts a damper on an opening day party like the building inspector unexpectedly appearing with orders to clear the building until the automatic sprinkler system has been tested and approved.

Summing Up

There's a lot going on while your building is going up. Trying to keep track of who is responsible for what, and if they are doing it, can be a full-time job. Let's summarize some of the major duties of the principal players. I am assuming that the building is being built as a conventional design/bid/build project. If it is not, some of the architect's and contractor's responsibilities may be merged.

Client's Responsibilities

☑ Obtain permits

The General Conditions may require you to obtain building and occupancy permits. The fees for these permits are often waived for publicly owned institutions.

☑ Prepare project financing

The client controls and administers the contract financing. Money must be available for payments to the contractor and architect as they are requested. The general timing of the payments is established in the preconstruction meeting. If the library's financing depends on property tax receipts, verify that your projected tax income will be available to the library when it is needed.

☑ Pay the contractor

The client is responsible for making payments to the contractor in accordance with the General Conditions of the contract. The client is contractually required to make the payments when they have been certified by the architect.

☑ *Review the architect's field reports and payment certifications*

Representatives of the client must review all the material submitted by the architect.

☑ *Maintain insurance*

The client must maintain insurance coverage as stipulated in the General Conditions of the contract. For publicly owned institutions, there may be minimum insurance requirements. The client is often responsible for liability insurance and property insurance. Discuss the options with your legal counsel and insurance carrier.

☑ *Attend progress and payout meetings*

Representatives of the client must attend all project meetings and should make reports to the board on a regular basis.

☑ *Stop work*

Only the client has authority to stop the work. In the event of a major problem, the architect can only advise you to issue a stop-work order. The architect cannot unilaterally issue a stop-work order.

☑ *Approve changes to the contract*

Any changes to the contract (i.e., change orders) must be thoroughly reviewed and approved. They should be submitted by the architect in a form that is easy for the layperson to understand.

☑ *Be familiar with the General Conditions of the contract*

The remainder of your responsibilities are spelled out in the General Conditions. Make sure that the building committee and project representative are familiar with them.

Architect's Responsibilities

The items listed below represent the minimum you can expect from your architect on a typical project. Exact responsibilities vary in accordance with the General Conditions of the contract and the Owner/Architect agreement.

☑ *Observe construction*

The architect is responsible for periodically "observing" the construction and advising the client of its progress and degree of conformance with the construction documents. I put "observe" in quotes because the AIA is very particular about this issue. The architect does not "inspect" or "approve" the construction, only "observes" it, to confirm that the work appears to be consistent with the contract documents.

Neither the architect nor the client can direct the contractor to perform the work in a certain manner. The final product is their primary concern, not the means of achieving it. Standard construction practice is that the "means and methods" of construction are entirely the responsibility of the contractor.

☑ *Prepare field reports*

The architect prepares field reports on the basis of observations at the job site. These should be submitted regularly to the board. Though not exhaustive, the field reports should be sufficiently detailed to record the status of the project.

☑ *Process contractor pay requests*

The architect must promptly process the contractor's pay requests. Both the contractor and the client are contractually bound to abide by the architect's decisions regarding payments to the contractor.

☑ *Impartially administer the construction contract*

The General Conditions require the architect to make impartial interpretations of the contract documents without bias toward either the contractor or the client.

☑ *Review shop drawings*

The architect reviews shop drawings for compliance with the contract documents and rejects or modifies those judged unacceptable.

☑ *Clarify the contract documents*

When inconsistencies or omissions are discovered in the contract documents, the architect issues clarifications as required. If these result in a significant change to either the scope or timing of the work, the changes are issued in the form of change orders.

☑ *Prepare change orders*

The architect prepares any needed change orders and advises the client of the appropriateness of the contractor's proposed costs for the additional work.

☑ *Prepare the punch list*

As a final part of construction observation, the architect prepares the punch list to advise the client of items not completed in accordance with the construction documents.

Contractor's Responsibilities

Beyond the actual construction of the building, the contractor has several project management responsibilities. Many of them are administrative and are required by the General Conditions of the contract.

☑ *Provide a schedule for construction*

By the time of the preconstruction meeting, the contractor should prepare and submit a proposed schedule for the project. This is important in helping the client schedule payments to the contractor.

☑ *Supply waivers and proof of insurance*

The contractor should supply lien waivers and certificates of insurance. These are usually required in the General Conditions. Have the architect, your attorney, and your insurance carrier review these documents to verify that the interests of the library are being protected.

☑ *Submit as-built documents*

No building is built exactly as it is drawn. Whether because of change orders or unforeseen events, there are always some deviations to the original documents. At the close of the project, the contractor or architect should prepare a set of record drawings documenting how the building actually went together. These drawings are especially important for documenting the locations of items that are concealed within walls or under floor slabs. If the changes are small, they may be recorded as markups on one of the architect's original sets of drawings. Whatever their form, these "as-built" drawings should be submitted to the client.

Before You Go . . .

There are a few more things the contractor should give you before packing up. It's easy to overlook some of these details in the excitement of completing the project. Many of them are itemized in the specifications. Ask the architect to review them with you to help you determine what you should be getting. Here are some of the more common ones:

☑ *Guarantees and warranties*

The specifications call for many items to have warranties beyond the standard one-year general warranty for the building. Most of these have a written warranty issued by the manufacturer or dealer. The general contractor should assemble all the specified warranties and give them to you.

☑ *Additional materials*

The specifications usually require the contractor to reserve a specified percentage of certain materials and finishes used on the project and deliver them to the client on completion. This is especially important for items that are custom colored or manufactured in lots that may be difficult to match at a later date. This list includes things like floor tiles, paint, wall coverings, and ceiling tiles.

☑ *Keys*

Check the specifications and find out how many keys the contractor is required to supply you, and see that they are properly labeled.

☑ *Training*

The contractor is often required to provide library personnel with training in the operation and maintenance of systems and equipment installed as a part of the construction contract. This includes everything from the operation of sophisticated mechanical systems to cleaning instructions for vinyl flooring.

☑ *Manuals*

The contractor should assemble and submit the manuals with the operating and maintenance instructions for equipment installed in your new building. Manuals should be provided for heating and ventilating systems, security systems, and all other electronic and mechanical systems. Instructions for the care and maintenance of landscaping materials should also be provided.

☑ *Landscape materials*

A quantity of grass seed and other landscape materials should be provided to the client. In practice, most landscape materials are covered under the one-year building guarantee, so the contractor is responsible for replacing any plants that do not make it through the first seasonal cycle.

☑ *Cleanup*

At the close of the project, just before the client takes occupancy, the contractor should thoroughly clean the premises, including the site. A contractor's crew should scour the building from top to bottom, cleaning up paint spatters and drywall dust, cleaning windows, picking up loose nails on the roof deck, and generally making the place spotless. After substantial completion, the library's staff is responsible for cleaning and general maintenance of the property.

Moving In

After months of construction and many, many project meetings, your building is beginning to look like a library; it may even resemble the design presentation drawings your architect showed you so long ago. If you've spent a lot of time at the job site, you have probably learned quite a bit about how a building is put together. You may have watched as the first excavations were made, as the foundations were poured, and as the structural steel was erected. You may have seen masons, electricians, and carpenters working side by side and wondered how they kept out of each other's way.

Thousands of parts were brought to the site and somehow assembled to make a building that beforehand was only an abstraction on paper. The most satisfying part of it is that you have played a role in the development of that idea. Your architect may have guided the design effort, but your decisions and input are embodied in the building you see before you.

There eventually comes a day when everything is far enough along that you can move in and begin operations. If you've ever moved into a new house, you have some idea of what this is like: boxes everywhere, painters and electricians hurrying to finish their work, library staff arranging furniture, and moving vans shuttling back and forth.

YOUR NEW BUILDING. You probably know your building inside and out; you've made uncounted visits to the job site and attended the birth of your new library. Something's different now. It may suddenly strike you that this is no longer a "job site"; it is your new building. Take a few moments to savor it.

Smell is the most evocative of senses. Nothing brings back distant memories better than the experience of a once-familiar smell. For me, the smells of new carpeting and fresh paint with undertones of wax and furniture polish will always be linked with the excitement of moving into a new building. These smells may soon become memories. As our buildings become "greener" and incorporate more sustainable design principles, fewer and fewer materials are permitted to release chemical compounds into the air. Low VOC (volatile organic compound) paints and carpets will soon become the norm. This will result in healthier and more environmentally sustainable buildings. I discuss this in more depth in chapter 13.

And now the matchless deed's achiev'd, Determin'd, dar'd and done.

—Christopher Smart

GETTING TO KNOW YOU. New ships are taken on a shakedown cruise to work out the bugs. Your first few months in a new building are the library's version of a shakedown cruise. You can expect to remain in regular contact with your architect and the contractor for at least a year while the building is being fine-tuned. Ventilating systems will need to be adjusted, balky door hardware fixed, and minor roof leaks repaired.

The one-year guarantee on your new building is intended to account for the minor items that weren't caught on the punch list. There may be legal recourse available should a major flaw in the construction become apparent after the one-year guarantee expires. If this happens, you should discuss the matter with your architect and the library's legal counsel. The laws protecting you in this eventuality vary from state to state.

STOP THE PRESSES! Even if you sponsored an event to commemorate the groundbreaking, this is the time for a real celebration. Get your most creative staff members to work on ways to get the public involved in a library open house. You might consider a kid's art contest, a dog show, or a tour of the library for the media. Maybe a last section or two of sidewalk in an unobtrusive place could be poured during the festivities and local kids invited to put their handprints in it. It really doesn't matter what you do, as long as it gets the public to your new library. And, as before, get the newspaper people there. Cajole, bribe, or threaten them until they agree to give your event the coverage you know it deserves. With a little publicity, you should be able to instill in the community the same feeling of pride as you have in their new library.

Chapter 10

Postconstruction

It ain't over 'til it's over.

—Yogi Berra

Readers who are parents may remember the first time they were alone with their first child. We had our child at home. There was a nurse-midwife and a doctor in attendance. They had seen it all many times before and had quick, expert answers for nearly any question that occurred to a nervous parent. We were lucky; after the nurse and doctor left, there were in-laws and friends there to give advice and lend support. The time came, however, when the last in-law packed up to go home and friends departed for their own families. After waving good-bye to the last of our helpers, we closed the front door and looked at each other. We were left with two things, a new baby and the inevitable question: What do we do now?

You've lived and worked in buildings your whole life. But a new building, that's a little different. Like being a first-time parent, there's a lot to learn. Fortunately, there is help if you need it. When my wife and I took stock of our situation, we realized that we had two important resources at our disposal—a borrowed copy of Dr. Spock and a telephone. The professional team that helped deliver your new building will not just pack up and leave when you occupy the facility. Their expertise is still available to you to help you work out the bugs and make everything in your new building work as it was intended. When the boiler goes out on the first really cold day, or the fire alarm repeatedly goes off for no apparent reason, or the front door opens of its own volition every time the wind comes out of the north, help is as close as your telephone and that thick binder of maintenance manuals the contractor should have turned over to you at the close of construction.

Most postconstruction architectural services are not included in the Owner/ Architect agreement. They thus fall under the heading of "additional services." As additional services, the scope of the services and the architect's compensation for those services should be worked out in advance. In this chapter, we look at services you can expect the architect to provide as a part of a basic contract, and those that you might elect to add to the your contract. The "shopping list" of additional postconstruction services in this chapter can be used as a starting point for discussions between the board and architect as you decide which ones might fit your situation.

What You Can Expect to Be Included

Most AIA Owner/Architect contracts stipulate that the architect's services conclude at the time of the issuance of the final certificate of payment to the contractor, or sixty days after substantial completion, whichever comes first. After that point, you could be billed for additional work on the part of the architect. The number of postconstruction services the architect is willing to provide as part of the basic agreement depends to a large degree on your relationship with the architect, your preferences, and your in-house capabilities. Discuss these items with your architect at the beginning of the project, while you are working out the contract to make sure that everyone has the same expectations.

As a minimum, you can expect the architect to provide the following services after you take possession of your new building:

COORDINATING THE FINAL CLOSEOUT. We discussed final closeout services in chapter 9. I mention them here because some of them might be "postconstruction" in the sense that they can occur after you have moved into your new building. These services include everything that is required to close out the construction contract and issue the final payment to the contractor. Punch lists, record drawings, and final cleanup are monitored to ensure that the contractor has provided you with everything included in the contract for construction. These services are usually included under the basic agreement between you and your architect.

CORRECTING DESIGN FLAWS. Should any minor problems arise because of flaws in the design of your building, the architect should consult with you and provide services as required to rectify them. From the point of view of risk management, and in the interest of maintaining good client relations, the architect is usually happy to work with you to straighten out any design-related problems. Thus, if the staff lounge is too cold, or if there is an area of the reading room with an unacceptably low level of illumination, the architect should coordinate any modifications required to make things right.

Because of the growing complexity of modern buildings, it is not unusual for problems to crop up in the mechanical and electrical systems. Systems that were previously simple, stand-alone arrangements are increasingly linked electronically to enhance building safety and energy efficiency. The architect and consultants are frequently called in to adjust or modify building systems to get them running within the specifications. When we consider sustainable architecture in chapter 13, we will look at building commissioning—a formalized process to ensure that everything within your building was installed correctly and is running as is should.

Optional Postconstruction Services

"You get what you pay for" is a significant theme when it comes to selecting your architect. Many postconstruction services are not explicitly included in the standard Owner/Architect contract, and the number of "additional" services you receive without additional fees depends on your relationship with your architect. If you select your architect primarily by price shopping, you can expect that the lower-priced architects are cutting back somewhere. Postconstruction services are frequently scaled back by an architect looking to reduce the professional fee. If you are comparing the proposed services of several architects, be sure their proposals include similar scopes of postconstruction assistance.

Before beginning a project, it is difficult to estimate the value of an architect's postconstruction services. If everything goes smoothly and you have a good contractor, few services may be required after you take occupancy of the building. If the picture isn't so rosy, you and the architect may be seeing a lot of each other. This may result in some significant and unexpected bills unless compensation was agreed on beforehand.

Here are some other commonly offered postconstruction services. As additional services, the prices for each should negotiated as a part of the client/architect contract. There is space at the end of the standard AIA contract for identifying the scope and cost of additional services. Some of these services are typically provided shortly after taking occupancy of the building; others imply a long-term relationship between architect and client.

☑ *Mechanical and electrical changes*

After you've been in your building for some time, you may identify changes you would like made to the mechanical and electrical systems. Maybe some new computers generate more heat than was anticipated, additional security lighting is required around the building, or more electrical outlets are needed to accommodate new equipment. If the change is simple, like a few additional electrical outlets, you could hire a local electrician to make the changes. For additional site lighting or major adjustments to a cooling system, it might be appropriate to retain the architect to coordinate the work and ensure that you get the most for your money.

☑ *Scheduling the move*

Complicated moves can require some intensive scheduling and logistical work to bring everything off smoothly. With a detailed knowledge of the building schedule and of how you operate, the architect is well placed to aid you in coordinating your move. The architect can work with the moving company to design an efficient strategy for the move that minimizes both your downtime and your aggravation. The more critical your schedule, the more you should consider retaining the architect to assist in coordinating the move.

☑ *Coordination and check of record drawings*

There is considerable variation in the quality of as-built drawings prepared by building contractors. After your building is finished, an accurate set of as-built drawings will be an invaluable resource. Here's an example:

I once was the structural engineer for a project in a large city in which the owners asked us to determine if their disused 1920s-era department store building could be transformed into (believe it or not) a multistory parking garage. None of the original drawings could be located, so we set to the task of determining the structural capacity of the old building. The building's frame was made of concrete. To determine its strength, we were going to have to literally jackhammer portions of it apart to find out the sizes and spacing of the steel reinforcing bars within.

We began by measuring the building. One day, after about a week of work in the cold and echoing interior, I was measuring the elevator penthouse and discovered a complete set of as-built drawings where they had fallen behind an old desk. That discovery saved us weeks of work, and the owners tens of thousands of dollars.

This is admittedly an extreme example. The chances of you wanting to convert your library into a parking garage are probably pretty slim. There is, however, a fairly good possibility that an addition or substantial remodeling will be done in the future. An accurate set of as-built drawings is an insurance policy against unpleasant and potentially expensive surprises. A common problem is uncertainty about the true sizes and locations of existing footings and other underground structures. This is particularly a concern when attaching an addition to an existing building, when an unanticipated footing or underground utility can be a serious setback. Other kinds of as-built information that can be useful later are the color selections and names of the manufacturers for finish materials such as wallpaper, paint and carpeting, bricks, and door hardware.

It is particularly important that the as-built drawings reflect design changes that followed change orders and other modifications made during construction, since these do not appear on the original construction documents. If you wish, the architect can check and assemble the record documents to make sure the information the contractor provides is accurate, complete, and usable.

In addition, record documents must be updated from time to time over the life of the building to record the inevitable changes. Even an architect not involved with each new project can continue to update the drawings on a regular basis to keep them current. In the age of computer-aided drafting, this task is becoming easier than ever. In previous times, as-built architectural documents became palimpsests of erasures and redrawing. Rather than relying on old, yellowed pieces of tracing paper bearing the marks of years of modification, the computerized architect makes the required changes to a digital file and prints out a new drawing sheet to replace the previous version.

☑ Ten-month building inspection and warranty review

When the substantial completion paperwork is signed, the clock begins ticking on the warranties and guarantees that cover your building. Many of those warranties expire after one year, including the whole building warranty provided by the general contractor. I recommend that you consider hiring the architect to make a thorough inspection of the building ten months after substantial completion. In ten months your building will have undergone a nearly complete seasonal cycle, and many of the problems caused by thermal expansion and contraction will have become apparent. After a thorough inspection of the structure, the architect should put together what is essentially a punch list of items that must be fixed by the contractor under the terms of the whole building warranty. The architect can then observe the work to verify that it is done according to the contract. As in the construction period, the architect should issue field reports to the board to keep them informed of the progress of the work.

While the contractor is busy with any work covered under the whole building warranty, the architect can assemble all the other component warranties that come with your building and have each item checked out to verify that it is functioning as intended. Equipment manufacturers or their local suppliers often come to the site to do a warranty inspection. Sometimes it is automatic, and sometimes you have to ask for the inspection. The architect can coordinate this process to help you identify and get any services you are due.

☑ Long-term planning

After you move into your new library, you will undoubtedly discover things you wish you had done differently. Some of them can be addressed by adapting your procedures; others may call for changes in the building plan or equipment. The library director should always have a long-term capital improvement plan to accommodate the changing needs and situation of the library. Some new requirements may come from outside the library, such as those required by the ADA—an example of federal legislation requiring libraries to make changes to their facilities. The architect can help the library director identify potential projects and analyze their feasibility. This process resembles the programming phase that began your project. Using interviews and other data-gathering techniques, the architect assists you in identifying your present and future needs and in setting appropriate goals.

Your architect can suggest additional postconstruction services particularly suited to your needs. Many of these services need not be determined when the contract is signed with the architect; they can be provided later, on an as-needed basis. The provider can be the original architect for your building, or another if there was some dissatisfaction with the original arrangement. That brings us to another important "record document" that can be of some use to you as well as other libraries in your area: your post-project evaluation.

Evaluating the Project

After the project is completed and all the contracts are closed out, you may wish to assemble the involved staff and board members for a debriefing session. At a debriefing, you can discuss the successes, mistakes, and lessons learned during the long process of planning and constructing a new building. This is the time to frame as objective an evaluation as possible of your architect and of the relative success of your project. If you are contemplating additional projects—branch libraries, for example—this sort of evaluation could be utilized so that the lessons learned during this project are applied to the next.

The success of a project can be difficult to determine. No building is everything you wish it could be. A thousand small, and sometimes not so small, compromises have to be made to make a building a reality in the light of financial realities, site restrictions, and conflicting program requirements. The more you were involved in the process, the greater will be your understanding of the decisions that had to be made en route.

The Building

There are a few objective evaluations you can make of the tangible product of your enterprise. Many comments are, by their nature, more subjective. The evaluations can be discussed and the conclusions noted. A scorecard could also be developed to aid in your evaluation. Here are some of the questions that should be considered:

1. Was the building completed on time? If not, were the delays attributable to a particular player or were they out of anyone's control? Bad weather, labor strikes, and unforeseeable project conditions can delay even the best-run projects.

2. Was the cost of the building within the stated budget, including contingencies?

3. Were substantial change orders required? "Substantial" in this case might be defined as anything over 7 percent or so of the anticipated cost of the project for a new building. For an addition or remodeling, the percentage of the change orders might be higher.

4. Were all the original program requirements met?

5. "Is everyone happy?" You couldn't ask a more subjective question. It is, however, guaranteed to spur some discussion.

6. Do the patrons like it? If there are valid criticisms, record them for discussion with the architect.

7. Were the design goals met, and did they prove to be appropriate?

8. Is the building what you were expecting, or were you surprised at the end product?

The Architect

The architect can be evaluated in terms of both the perceived success of the project and the service provided. Some of these questions necessarily overlap those given above.

1. Did the architect provide all the services specified in the contract?
2. During the programming phase, was the data collected efficiently and were the program requirements satisfied in the end product?
3. Did the architect make appropriate use of materials provided by the library building consultant (if any)?
4. Was the architect responsive when you had questions or needed clarifications?
5. Was the architect willing to modify the design when so requested?
6. Was the building produced on budget and in time?
7. Was the increase in building costs because of change orders less than 7 percent of the initial bid amount?
8. If the answer to the previous two questions is no, was it because of poor service on the part of the architect?
9. Did the architect provide leadership in the design and building process?
10. Were the architect's budget estimates realistic?
11. Were the architect's estimates of the time required for construction realistic?
12. Did the architect adequately represent the library in negotiations with civil and municipal authorities?
13. Did the architect adequately represent the library in dealings with the contractor?
14. Was the architect easy to work with? Did he or she give due attention to your needs?
15. Was the total of the professional fees paid to the architect consistent with what you were led to expect?
16. Do you feel that you received good value for the money you spent for professional services?
17. Is the building, considering necessary compromises, what you wanted?
18. Would you use this architect again?

The questions on this list may sound something like those you would ask while selecting an architect. Many of them are, and we make use of this material when we discuss how to hire an architect in chapter 11.

The Library Organization

The ultimate success of your project depended, to a large degree, on the library staff and board of directors. There are a few questions that you should ask yourselves to help evaluate your own performance.

1. Did the in-house chain of command work effectively and efficiently?
2. If the answer to the above question is no, what would you do differently next time?

3. Did you respond promptly when the architect had questions or needed clarifications?

4. Were disagreements within the in-house project team resolved effectively?

5. Was the information provided by the library building consultant useful in the programming of the building?

6. Was the original financial planning done by the library staff and consultants valid?

7. Was the library prompt in obtaining insurance and permits as required by the contract?

8. Were requests for payment by the contractor honored promptly

9. Does the library have the in-house expertise to maintain and operate the mechanical and electrical systems in the new building?

10. Did the staff and members of the building committee give the project the time it deserved?

Problems and Pointing Fingers

A debriefing is one way of summarizing the project and putting the construction phase behind you. It marks the end of what may have been a two- or three-year journey. If the project went smoothly, the final punch list and closeout probably also went well. There are times, however, when those last few items on the punch list seem never to be completed, or when defects start showing up right after you occupy the building. That last payment to the contractor, the one that isn't made until the items on the punch list are completed, is usually enough of an incentive to guarantee that the work will be completed. But what happens when problems aren't apparent until after the contractor has cashed the final check, or if you think they may be due to faulty design on the part of the architect?

Discussing the subject of problems in the design of a building makes me acutely aware that I am wearing (at least) two hats here. As an architect, I want to say, "Take it easy on the designer; everybody makes mistakes." As a library trustee, I want to advise you to obtain satisfaction wherever you can to ensure that the taxpayers are getting their money's worth. One hat that I'm definitely not wearing is that of an attorney. Whenever there is a question of payment for damages, the library should discuss the matter with its legal counsel. Every problem has to be examined in its own light. Unfortunately, it's easier to point a finger than to solve a problem, and finger pointing often begins before the problem is even defined.

Identifying the problem is the first and perhaps the most important task. There are so many possibilities that we can't hope to go over enough examples to be a useful guide to solving your own construction-related problems. The best I can do here is to offer some advice that might help you define a problem. Once a problem is defined, a solution often suggests itself.

Aside from improper use by the client, postconstruction problems can be grouped into two rough categories—problems related to faulty design and those related to defective construction. This grouping implies distinct divisions of responsibility. In reality, things are seldom so clear-cut.

Design Flaws—Continued

The assessment of responsibility for shortcomings in the design of a building can be difficult. This gets back to the uncomfortable question of "who pays" posed when we were discussing change orders. There are two general kinds of design flaw—those that compromise part of the building program and make the building less useful, and those that might result in an unsafe condition and contribute to the chances of an accident or injury.

The first kind of design problem might be illustrated by the following example. Say that your library is substantially complete and you're beginning to move in. The library driver delivers the bookmobile from its former home at the old building to the new garage. Just before she pulls the vehicle in, someone notices that the top of the bookmobile is several inches higher than the underside of the garage door. You could argue that the architect should have been aware of the size of the vehicle and should be responsible for the cost of the required modifications to the garage.

If, in a different example, the bookmobile was purchased new and turns out to be too large for the door opening, you would be faced with some different questions. First, was the architect aware that the garage was intended to house a bookmobile? If so, did the library make the measurements available to the architect in time to incorporate them into the design? Maybe the library staff did not know the dimensions of the bookmobile when the building was being designed. You still might ask if the door height is sufficient to clear the "typical" bookmobile. If it could be demonstrated that the door is large enough for the average bookmobile, and that the library had purchased one that was unusually tall, the architect could say that the difficulty arose through the library's failure to supply the designer needed information.

The best thing that you, the client, can do to avoid bearing the responsibility for this kind of dilemma is to be sure that your needs are effectively expressed to the architect during the programming and design phases of the project. The success of this depends largely on how well your in-house team is organized and managed. A good architect should identify most of the building requirements by asking questions during the programming phase. That does not, however, relieve the client of the responsibility of identifying special items the architect might miss, and of transmitting that information to the architect. Another thing to remember is that the library board signed off on the plans during the design phase. An architect cannot realistically expect laypeople to go over a set of building plans with a fine-tooth comb and identify every potential shortcoming, but this does illustrate the importance of the milestone reviews and of the client's responsibility for thoroughly examining the drawings before approving them.

Design flaws that might result in an accident or injury are always a cause for concern, and perhaps a reason for immediate action. The aim of the architect is to give you the building you want. Whatever your requirements, it is the duty of the architect to design the building in such a way that it promotes the health, safety, and welfare of the public. You rely on the architect's professional expertise to produce a safe building while fulfilling the objectives expressed in the building program. There is also the additional safety net provided by building codes, which typically set the minimum standards of safety for your building. You assume that the architect is familiar with the applicable codes and that your building will conform to them.

Many potentially serious design flaws are not, however, covered by building codes. This is where you have to depend on the architect's experience and common sense. A dangerous flaw might be as simple as improper grading adjacent to a sidewalk which causes water to run over the walk during a rain. By itself, this condition is not particularly dangerous. Combine it with freezing temperatures, however, and you have a situation in which someone could fall and be injured. If the grading was done per the construction documents, the architect may bear some responsibility in case of an accident.

The degree of the architect's responsibility for fixing design flaws depends on several things. First, the design of the item in question must have been included in the architect's contract. If the client had a direct contract with a security company to install a burglar alarm system for the new building, the architect bears no responsibility if the system fails to function as advertised. Second, the problem must not have arisen through faulty maintenance on the part of the library. This is especially important when it comes to complex mechanical systems. Finally, the usage creating the problem must be something that would reasonably be inferred by the architect. If the library staff suspends a heavy display from the suspended ceiling grid and the grid sags, the architect would have no responsibility for the condition unless originally instructed by the client to design the grid to support additional loads.

Before laying blame for what is assumed to be a design problem, schedule a meeting with the architect to discuss the matter. What may at first seem to be a design omission might later prove to be the result of a miscommunication within the project team. In the event that someone claims that a design error causes an injury, or in case of disasters like structural failures, many states allow the library to take legal action against the architect—at least until the expiration of the statute of limitations. As always, the library's lawyer should be consulted.

Construction Flaws

Everyone has heard of construction failures. Most of them are not dramatic—leaky roofs, cracked foundation walls, doors that don't close, and windows that won't open. On occasion, television news shows pictures of a building that suffered a catastrophic collapse. Such failures are rare in the United States thanks to the enforcement of building codes and the overall quality of construction here.

A leaky roof or a cracked foundation wall on your building will probably not make the six o'clock news, but it is important to you. The real question is what to do about it. Whatever the problem, the first thing to do is to try to identify the cause and determine if it is covered under a warranty. If there is warranty coverage, you can contact the contractor and schedule the required repairs. Remember that the entire building is typically covered under a one-year warranty, and some components like roofs and mechanical equipment may be covered for longer periods.

If the problem occurs after the expiration of the one-year building warranty and is not covered by an individual warranty, you may have several options. Let's assume, as an example, that the problem was caused by faulty construction and not by poor maintenance or something reaching the end of its anticipated lifespan. First, call the contractor and describe the situation. If the contracting company has an ongoing relationship with the library, it may come out and make the fix at its own cost in the interest of maintaining good relations with a valued client. If the contractor claims that your problem is not the result of faulty construction, or refuses to make repairs without charging the library, you may have to turn to the architect to assist you in demonstrating that the work did not meet the specifications.

Showing that part of a building was not built according to the construction documents can be difficult. Sometimes investigating this is invasive in the sense that portions of the building have to be removed to gain access to the component in question. It might be as easy as lifting up some ceiling tiles to expose a steel beam to verify that the correct size beam was installed. If your concrete foundation wall is cracking, it is a relatively simple matter to have the concrete tested to verify that its strength is up to specifications. If you are questioning whether the contractor put the proper amount of reinforcing steel inside the concrete wall, it will require a more thorough (and hence more expensive) investigation.

If you wind up in the situation of having to hire someone to verify beam sizes to check up on a contractor's work, you may find yourself questioning the value of the architect's job site observations. It is worth repeating that the purpose of the architect's field observations is not to ferret out every construction flaw but rather to confirm general compliance with the contract documents. There are so many things going on simultaneously at a construction site that it is virtually impossible to guarantee that everything has been built exactly according to the plans. Engaging a full-time field representative does not eliminate problems with poor construction, but it can help reduce the chances of a serious shortcoming.

There is always the potential for a disagreement between the contractor and the architect in establishing the liability for poor construction. Not surprisingly, this often takes the form of each insisting that the other is responsible. The architect may maintain that the problem is a matter of faulty construction, and the contractor may declare that it is the result of poorly drawn or detailed architectural documents. If no agreement can be reached, expert third-party opinions may be needed and the matter settled in the courts. Get the library's attorney involved if you are in the position of having to demonstrate poor workmanship on the part of a contractor. The rules for documenting your investigations can be very specific, and they vary from state to state. Depending on the laws in your state, your protection against faulty construction could extend up to, and perhaps beyond, the statute of limitations.

Back to the Beginning

We have come a long way in these pages. We began by discussing the need for the client to understand the architect's vocabulary and then looked at each part of a "typical" architectural project. You've learned what happens during each phase of the undertaking. At this point, you have an overview of the kinds of service architects provide, and at least a general idea of what you can expect them to do for you.

There is another important part of the process, one that occurs before your project is begun. In the next chapter we discuss, not architectural services themselves, but rather who is going to provide those services and how you should go about finding and selecting your architect.

Chapter 11

Finding, Selecting, and Hiring an Architect

It was July 2, 1937, and the U.S. Coast Guard cutter *Itasca* was anchored off Rowland Island, the northernmost island of the Phoenix Island group in the South Pacific. The *Itasca* and her crew were waiting for Amelia Earhart. Amelia and her navigator, Fred Noonan, were on one of the last legs of a record-breaking trip around the world. They were flying over the Pacific and they were lost.

In his prime, Noonan had been one of the best navigators around. He was a chief navigator for Pan American when the airline established its China Clipper service across the Pacific. He was also an alcoholic, and the years of hard living had taken their toll. By the time of Amelia's around-the-world attempt he was, perhaps, no longer the right man for the job. Seeing this, many of her friends had advised her against using him.

At Rowland Island the radiomen aboard the *Itasca* could hear Amelia as she tried to contact them. Because of inappropriate radio equipment aboard the plane and a lack of coordination between her and the Coast Guard, she could not hear their replies. "We are circling but cannot hear you . . ." she called. According to Noonan's calculations they should have been right over Rowland, but there was nothing below but ocean. Over and over, Amelia called the *Itasca*. The radiomen could hear the frustration in her voice as her fuel supply ran low. Eventually, her transmissions ceased. An extensive search failed to come up with any trace of the aircraft.

Amelia has always been one of my heroines; I was surprised to learn that poor planning had so much to do with her disappearance.

Navigation is a tricky thing. Over a long trip, the consequences of even a small error can grow until you are far from your intended position. It takes knowledge and care to do it right. An architect has much in common with a navigator. In each project, the architect is presented with a destination and is expected to find the path of least resistance to attain it. Based on personal research and experience, an architect may even advise that the ultimate goal be reconsidered. In the end, however, it is the client who decides. Selecting the right navigator is an important part of planning your journey. In this chapter, we see a method for finding and selecting an architect, along with suggestions on negotiating fees and contracts. As with all journeys, good preparation is everything.

I find the great thing in this world is not so much where we stand, as in what direction we are moving.
—Oliver Wendell Holmes

The winds and the waves are always on the side of the ablest navigators.
—Edward Gibbon

Without a Clue

We recently had a request for qualifications (RFQ) arrive in our office. Because they represent potential work, RFQs are always welcome and we respond to them immediately. This proposal was from a nearby municipality that wished to construct several new buildings in an existing park as well as develop the site by providing new electrical service, sewers, and a well.

There were brief descriptions of each building and a list of architectural services that were to be included. The list contained many of the services we have been looking at in the preceding chapters. Here's what they were seeking:

1. Programming to identify space requirements.
2. Preparation of alternative designs and budgets.
3. Preparation of a final design and budget.
4. Permit applications.
5. Construction observation.

It seemed pretty straightforward so far.

The RFQ asked us to submit our qualifications, resumes of key personnel, and professional fees, with the fees broken down for each phase of the work. The first alarm bells went off when we got to the part requesting fees. Although the work was outlined in broad terms, the brief descriptions of the buildings weren't enough for us to begin estimating the time it would take us to design and draw them. In addition, there were no clues that we could use to evaluate the magnitude of the civil engineering work it would take to supply the site with water, sewer, and electricity. Were existing sewers and waterlines close by and easy to connect to, or were they a half mile away on the other side of a federally protected wetland?

The request for fees presented another problem. In many states, including ours, most public bodies are either prohibited or discouraged from requesting professional fees from architects in an RFQ. We look at this later when we discuss qualifications-based selection.

Our dilemma was twofold. Should we inform the municipality that they were violating the law in requesting fees and possibly get the reputation of being a "squeaky wheel," and thus potentially lose our chance of being selected, or should we ignore the regulation and proceed with our response in the hope that we would be the low bidder? The second choice came with the added potential that someone could legally challenge our contract with the city as being illegal and have us pulled off the job, possibly without being compensated for services we may have provided to that point. We decided to proceed cautiously until we could evaluate the situation.

When we called the contact person at the city with our questions about the size of the project, we found that he didn't have any estimates of the proposed budget or eventual square footage of the buildings. Furthermore, no one had any information regarding existing utilities or of the potential problems in getting them to the project site. We were now in the position of having to put a lot of up-front time into evaluating the feasibility of the project and the site conditions in order to come up with a realistic fee.

Our dilemma was finally resolved when we got our contact at the city to admit that the city fathers were planning to spend "around $150,000" on the project. We realized that, with all the unknowns, we might easily spend the potential fee for a project this size in doing the up-front work required to put together our proposal. It looked like a lose-lose situation. If we weren't selected, we would be in the red for the substantial amount of money we spent trying to define their project. If we were selected, the fee would probably be barely enough to recoup our up-front expenses, not to mention paying us for the programming, design work, and construction documents.

We decided to write the city a letter thanking them for their interest in us but declining to submit a proposal.

This story might remind you of the reroofing project we looked at back in chapter 2. You have to know which questions to ask and what information to give if you want to get a high-quality product.

The process of hiring an architect can be broken into seven basic steps. For public institutions, some of the details differ from one state to another. Always ask your lawyer to inform you of any local requirements. Before you even consider construction, you will have to debate one of the first issues raised in this book: Is this trip really necessary? If you are convinced that it is, read on.

Step 1. Evaluate the Need for an Architect

If your project is a building or an addition, you are probably legally required to hire a licensed architect. For smaller projects this is often something of a judgment call. Weigh your in-house resources against the task. If you want to put up some knee walls to subdivide an area in the children's library and your building engineer is good at carpentry, you can probably skip hiring an architect. But even this project is not necessarily as simple as it sounds. The smallest of projects can still raise questions about required paths of egress for fire exiting and regulations on the use of combustible materials in construction. If you're considering reroofing or spending $100,000 on new carpeting, I strongly advise you to hire an architect to write specifications and oversee the bidding process. One additional test you could apply in evaluating the need for an architect involves building permits. If the project you are planning requires a permit, there is a good chance that drawings or calculations must be produced by a licensed architect or engineer.

Consider the professional fees on smaller projects to be "expert insurance" that can provide a better finished product and also help insulate the library from potential liability. On some occasions, it is appropriate to hire engineering consultants directly without first hiring an architect. An example of this might be renovations to a boiler or plumbing system; for this kind of work, it is usually appropriate to hire a local mechanical/plumbing engineering firm.

Step 2. Determine the Scope of Services You Need

A thorough examination of your goals is the first stage in determining the services you want an architect to provide. A defined list of services helps ensure that the same standards are used in your evaluation of each of the potential architects and also aids you in the preparation of an RFQ.

You will have a head start if you are utilizing the services of a library building consultant. The document produced by the building consultant sets your initial course, for the consultant's research will identify many of your initial requirements. With the consultant's report in hand, there are several general questions you should consider:

1. What is lacking in your current facility?
2. Is expansion of your services a goal?
3. Is expansion of the size of your present facility a goal?
4. Which parts of your facility and what aspects of your services need to expand or be modified?
5. If you are contemplating an addition, which services will be housed in the new space?

6. Are there any time constraints associated with your project? For example, is your present library building scheduled for demolition because of municipal plans to widen a road or develop a new scheme for the city center? If there are scheduling requirements, plot them out; this will form the basis of a project time line.

7. At this time, do you intend only to test the waters with a feasibility study and an estimated cost for the work, or do you have to commit to design and build a new building or addition?

8. Does a referendum need to be passed for you to accomplish your goals?

9. Do you want continuous input into the design process from the architect, or will milestone reviews be sufficient?

Once these questions have been considered, you are ready to begin defining the scope of services you will itemize in your RFQ.

If you are not using a library building consultant, you may wish to hire an architect on a preliminary basis to prepare a building program. The services a library building consultant provides overlap to some degree with those an architect would ordinarily provide in assembling a building program. A library building consultant is an expert at programming libraries and can probably provide you with more detailed information than could an architect. Depending on your location and the specifics of your project, a library building consultant may not be required or even be available.

Remember that, although architects routinely produce building programs, programming is not a part of the basic services included in typical architectural contracts. It is an additional service that can be added to the scope of work defined in the client/architect contract. You could use a program developed by an architect to evaluate what services you require while you are preparing your RFQ. If this method is chosen, the architect could be retained on the understanding that the current relationship ends with the end of the building programming and that this architect would be among the group of architects considered at a later date for the remainder of the work. As an alternate possibility, there are individuals who bill themselves as building programmers rather than architects. If there are any of them in your area, they would be able to provide the same service.

In choosing a consultant to provide a building program, you could use a simplified version of the method for selecting an architect presented in this chapter. Previous experience in programming buildings of similar size and good references are of primary importance.

There are several advantages to having a building program in hand when you begin your search for the architect to design your building. One is that a potential architect gets a good idea of the size of the project and can fine-tune the scope and price of the proposed services. If you eliminate some of the uncertainties, the architect will not have to increase the fee arbitrarily to cover the unknowns, thus resulting in cost savings for the library. Another major advantage is that a building program is a large component of a feasibility study. Once you know the approximate size of the project, it is relatively easy to use some local costs per square foot for other buildings and get a rough idea of its potential cost.

Let's review the services you might need for a typical project. Though this book is primarily aimed at libraries, this information applies to almost any building type.

Appetizer: Predesign Services

PROGRAMMING. Programming is required to identify your needs accurately. This can be done by either a library building consultant, an architect, or a professional programmer. Programming may be done before the consultant for the remainder of the architectural project is selected. Note that, if the initial program is done by a library building consultant, additional architectural programming is required to cover items not included in the library consultant's report.

SITE ANALYSIS. Site analysis is required for almost any project that involves new construction or a building addition. An analysis may be performed for several different potential sites to aid the choice of one to purchase. Like programming, this is not part of the basic services and is often negotiated separately. Site analysis and programming are termed *predesign* services. Some architects may elect to include site analysis as a part of their basic services if you know which site you are going to use for your building. If part of the scope of work involves site selection, you probably have to pay for additional services.

FEASIBILITY STUDY. If you need general information about the potential for building a new library or an addition, you can commission an architect to perform a feasibility study. Site analysis and programming are often included as parts of a feasibility study. A three-part study consisting of programming, site analysis, and schematic building design (including a cost estimate) should be sufficient to give you a general indication of the viability of your project.

REFERENDUM ASSISTANCE. If a referendum is required to fund your project, you may wish to have the architect assist you by preparing visual displays and other materials to get your message out to the public. If the architect has a talent for public speaking, you may also be able to use those skills to your advantage. An architect who has been awarded a project that depends on a successful referendum may be willing to donate time to help you get your issue approved by the voters. If you want the architect to prepare renderings of what your building may look like, you may have to authorize continuation into the schematic design phase.

First Course: Building Design

SCHEMATIC DESIGN. Schematic design is an essential part of the process of designing a new building. The general layout and appearance of the building are defined during this time. If information about the building characteristics is important to your referendum effort, you may wish to have the architect complete the schematic design before launching your publicity drive. Schematic design can also be included as part of a thorough feasibility study. A schematic design enables the architect to generate a more accurate estimate of the construction cost of the building. If schematic design is included as a part of a feasibility study, the remainder of the architect's basic services could be made contingent on the passage of the referendum or the availability of funding. For our referendum-based projects we usually proceed through the schematic design phase and hold at that point until the referendum is passed. This is the case even if we have contracted with the client for a full scope of services.

DESIGN DEVELOPMENT. The schematic design is refined and developed into a complete building design during design development. At this stage the architect retains and coordinates the work of several consultants. Design development is usually not undertaken until funding for the project is secured.

Second Course: Construction Documents and Bidding

CONSTRUCTION DOCUMENTS. Preparing construction documents is the most time-consuming portion of an architect's contract. Construction documents are expensive and are not generally done unless project funding is assured. If project funding will not be available in the near future, you can consider delaying the construction documents phase until the time of construction is closer at hand. This also ensures that code changes that may have taken effect in the interim are accounted for on the drawings.

BIDDING. The architect assists throughout the bidding process, preparing bid forms, procuring bids, and answering contractor's questions. The analysis and evaluation of bids are also critical in awarding a contract. The architect or engineer who prepared the drawings should evaluate the bids and report to the board.

Third Course: Construction

There are several options with regard to administration of the construction contract:

CONSTRUCTION ADMINISTRATION BY THE ARCHITECT. For most projects, it makes sense to have the architect, the person most familiar with the building, oversee the administration of the construction contract. Construction administration is approximately 20 percent of an architect's contract in a standard arrangement. If you wish full-time representation on the site, you usually have to pay the architect additional professional fees.

CONSTRUCTION ADMINISTRATION BY A CONSTRUCTION MANAGER. For large or complex projects, you can retain a construction manager to oversee the work. This is often done as an alternative to full-time field observation by the architect. If you hire a construction manager, you still need to retain the architect during the construction phase to offer clarifications and make any required adjustments to the construction documents. See chapter 12 for a discussion of construction management.

IN-HOUSE CONSTRUCTION ADMINISTRATION. You can have your staff handle the construction administration if you have personnel with the required expertise. In this case, you may still wish to hire the architect for clarifications and adjustments. Be advised that construction administration can be very time consuming and requires a thorough knowledge of construction practices.

Dessert: Postconstruction

Postconstruction services are additional architectural services that can extend the architect's quality control beyond the close of the construction contract. Examples of common postconstruction activities by the architect are listed in chapter 10. These services do not need to be itemized when you negotiate the original contract with the architect. Rather than commit to a full range of postconstruction services early on, you can have the architect provide services on an as-needed basis, perhaps on an hourly rate. If you choose this option, have the architect submit a listing of the hourly rates that would be used when and if you require postconstruction services. You should not expect to pay the architect for postconstruction services that are clearly required because of a mistake or oversight on the part of the architect.

Step 3. Write the Request for Qualifications

Even if you are sure which architects you will interview for your project, you should write an RFQ, which helps standardize the procedures you use to interview and hire. After the board or evaluation committee has agreed on the scope of services required for the project, the preparation of the RFQ can begin. See appendix A for a sample RFQ. This format is just a suggestion. All that matters is that you cover the important information in a way that is clear and easy to understand.

There is always a question of whether you should request that fees be included as part of an architectural selection process. For the moment, let's ignore the possibility that it is illegal (as in most locales) to base architectural selection on fees and look instead at a fundamental problem with asking for architectural fee quotations up front.

When you take bids for the construction of a building, the contractors have the use of a detailed, comprehensive set of drawings and specifications that gives them the exact scope of work they are to perform. With the information presented to them, they can put together a quote that is profitable for them as well as competitive with the prices of the other contractors bidding on the work. A similarly detailed set of specifications does not usually exist when you are looking at purchasing architectural professional services. As soon as fees are requested, you can find yourself in the same boat as the unnamed municipality whose RFQ I mentioned at the beginning of this chapter. Unless you are very specific about the extent of services being requested and can give detailed information regarding the project, architects will always be somewhat in the dark about the number of hours it will take them to do the work and the number of tasks involved. There will also be a degree of uncertainty regarding the expectations of the client.

Library boards and directors are often inexperienced in the selection and hiring of professional consultants. The size of the professional fee may be the one thing they can pick out of a proposal and really understand. Unfortunately, although they may understand the fee, they often do not fully understand the services they are purchasing. Careful study and a well-written RFQ are your best preparation. Qualifications-based selection, which we look at shortly, provides a method for selecting professional services that is more sophisticated than merely looking for the lowest fee.

Step 4. Find Architects

This is the easy part. Even if the local architects haven't gotten wind of your building plans by the time you are writing your RFQ, it does not usually take much effort on your part to stimulate interest in your project. Though your office manager might be taking constant telephone calls from would-be applicants, you may still be required to advertise the fact that you are searching for an architect. Laws regulating if, and how, you must advertise your project differ from one state to another. Consult the library's attorney if you are unsure of the requirements in your case.

An additional way of finding interested architects is to turn to your file of marketing materials that architects and other consultants regularly send the library. (You are keeping that stuff, aren't you?) Many libraries have a continuously updated file in which such materials are kept on hand for a year and then discarded.

Institutions that maintain this kind of system often notify the architects on file that an RFQ is available. In some jurisdictions you are legally required to send the materials to anyone who has a letter of interest in your files.

The Devil You Know

If the library has successfully used a particular architectural firm in the past, that firm should be a candidate whether or not it currently has materials on file. Depending on local statutes, you may not even be required to evaluate other architects formally if you already have a satisfactory, ongoing relationship with a particular firm. If the project you envisage is much larger or radically different from those the previous firm handled, you may still want to consider a formal interview with that firm to determine if it is capable of the work and to verify that you feel comfortable with the selection.

If All Else Fails

In the unlikely event that you are having trouble finding architects, there are a few other possible sources:

LOCAL LIBRARIES. Look around for other libraries that have recently completed construction projects. They should be a good source for both names of architects and reviews of their performance.

SYSTEM AND STATE LIBRARIES. Some larger institutions maintain directories of consultants (including architects) who have been used by member libraries. The directories may also contain information regarding the quality of the services rendered.

LIBRARY BUILDING CONSULTANT. If you are using one, your library building consultant can probably recommend several architectural firms on the basis of prior experience.

LOCAL CHAPTERS OF THE AIA. The AIA can be a valuable resource to anyone looking for architectural services. Most chapters publish a directory of architects within their regions along with synopses of the specialties of the listed firms. As an impartial organization, the AIA can offer no opinions regarding the performance of the listed architects.

Limiting the Field

Thoroughly evaluating a stack of proposals can be a daunting task. Some libraries in populous areas limit the number of architects being considered to avoid dividing their attention among too many proposals. Several "filters" are commonly used. One is locality; limit the firms under consideration to those within a certain geographic area, the concept being that local firms can offer quicker and more complete service—especially during the construction phase. Another potential advantage is political. If you are trying to pass a referendum, having a local firm may be more "politically correct." It may also be more effective in swaying public opinion. This strategy assumes that the local pool of architects is big enough to offer a sufficient number of firms for comparison and that there are several architects with experience in library design.

When pursuing projects that are far from our office, our firm often teams with a local architect who provides on-site representation during the construction phase and otherwise assists us with coordination with local authorities and the like. This arrangement offers the best of both worlds: library design expertise and local presence.

The most common filter is a minimum limit on the firm's experience in designing libraries. There is no substitute for experience, and a firm with a background in library design will spend less time learning the ropes and more time coming up with the best solution for your needs. In the interest of fairness, it is better to publicly limit the field in the RFQ by setting some minimum qualifications, perhaps specifying a minimum number of libraries the firm previously designed.

The most radical form of limiting the field is to allow proposals by invitation only, which you do by developing a short list of architects and sending RFQs only to them.

All in all, careful consideration must be given to the concept of limiting the number of architects you consider. You must ask yourself, first, whether it is legal, and second, whether you are doing this to save the building committee some work or are convinced that it will promote the public good. Your attorney can answer the first question; the second may require some discussion among the board.

> ## A CAUTIONARY TALE
>
> We recently responded to an RFQ in which one of the requirements was that firms located more than 50 miles from the project site had to partner with a local architect and state in their proposal who they were teaming with. This made sense at first blush, but after the fact the client regretted that decision. The problem was that there were only two or three local architects, and not all of them had experience with public buildings, much less libraries. Distant architects immediately snapped up the few qualified local firms. Other out-of-town firms that may not have gotten wind of the RFQ right away had no one to team with and were left out of consideration. The result was that the library had a much smaller pool of qualified architects' qualifications to consider and lost a lot of leeway in the selection of the right architect for them.

Step 5. Interview Candidates

What to Do before the Interview

Interviews can be the most intense and interesting part of your search for an architect. There are two overriding considerations to keep in mind. The first is to make good use of your time with the architects. Do your preparation and have your questions ready. The architects may be writing some of the script, but you are directing the show. It is up to you to ensure that things run smoothly and that everyone gets a fair chance. The second consideration is consistency. Make sure that the same questions are asked and the same format followed for each interview. Without this control, a meaningful comparison is impossible. This is not to say that the whole procedure should be so rigid that the architect is not allowed any outlet for self-expression during the interview. Set aside a defined amount of time for each architect to use as he or she sees fit.

Arrive at the Short List

The important word here is "short." For most projects, three or four firms should be enough to give you a good cross section of the types of architect you are seeking. Interviewing more than four firms makes it exponentially more difficult to distinguish them after the fact.

To generate the short list, the building committee should examine each proposal. Many committees find it useful to rank each respondent with a point system. The advantage of point-based systems is that they remove some of the subjectivity from the selection process. The points can then be totaled and the top-ranking three or four firms selected for the short list. A secret ballot approach can be helpful because it elicits committee members' true opinions without undue influence

It is better to know some of the questions than all of the answers.

—James Thurber

from peer pressure from assertive fellow committee members. Spreadsheets can be used to tally the responses. Table 11-1 is an example of a spreadsheet that tallies responses and assigns a predetermined weighting to each category.

If you use a point system, the categories on which you rate each architect should reflect the priorities of the board. If you are building an addition, your ratings might reflect the quality of previous projects the architects list on their proposals. If your project involves a large degree of site planning, one of the ratings might measure demonstrated ability in this area. When deciding on facets of the architectural firms you wish to rate, it is important that they reflect questions asked on the RFQ. References should also be taken into account during short listing. I suggest that the same person or team contact the references so that this process is also standardized. A script of questions should be developed by the selection committee and used for each contact.

Let's assume that you have used a point system and come up with a short list of three firms to consider. There are still a few things to do before the interview.

Inform the Applicants

Inform all applicants of the results of your short list selection. At this stage, letters usually suffice. The firms that are moving on to the interviews should be given a schedule for the interview. Also indicate the format for the interview as well as any other items that will be required by the selection committee.

Check the References

Depending on the number of applicants, you can follow up on references before or after you have formulated the short list. Standardization is again important. Gener-

Table 11-1

Sample point-system evaluation

	Number of library projects (25%)	Quality of design (15%)	Professionalism of RFQ presentation (15%)	Experience with sustainable design (25%)	Did they answer the questions that we asked in the RFQ? (10%)	"Intangibles": Overall impression of RFQ presentation (10%)	Total (100%)
DesignHaus	5	4	4	0	4	4	3.25
ABC Architects	4	4	3	2	5	3	3.35
Arrow-Gant Associates	4	2	2	3	5	4	3.25
Fleesing, Yiu Partnership	0	1	1	0	5	4	1.20
XYZ Deeziners Ltd.	3	3	3	3	5	2	3.10

Rank each submittal by the above criteria using a range of 0–5, where 5 is the best. Multiply each score by the weighting percentage in the top row and add the result to the total column. Maximum number of potential points is 5.

ate a list of questions and run through them with each reference. After asking all your set questions, ask the references if there is anything else they would like to add. Keeping good notes is important. If you are visiting the references in person, it might be a good idea to have two members of the selection committee go along so they can compare notes afterward. I usually try to call several references in addition to the ones the architects give on their RFQ responses. It is usually easy to find other projects that were done by the prospective architects, and a little detective work can uncover appropriate references. As with any form of relationship, architects hit it off better with some clients than with others. Sometimes projects can come off without a hitch yet the client will give a less than enthusiastic response; sometimes the opposite is the case. Never put too much weight on any one reference; look for trends.

In chapter 10 we looked at a list that could help you evaluate the service your architect gives you. When put to the architect's references, these same questions can help you evaluate the service that architect has given other clients. The list can be used as a starting point. Modify it as appropriate for your circumstances.

1. Did the architect provide all the services specified in the contract?

2. During the programming phase, was the data collected efficiently and were the program requirements met in the end product?

3. Did the architect make appropriate use of materials provided by the library building consultant (if any)?

4. Was the architect responsive when you had questions or needed clarifications?

5. Was the architect willing to modify the design when requested to do so by the board?

6. Was the building produced on budget and in time? If not, was this attributable to the architect?

7. Did change orders during construction increase the cost of the building by a significant amount? If so, were the changes caused by errors or oversights by the architect?

8. Did the architect provide leadership in the design and building process?

9. Were the architect's budget estimates realistic?

10. Were the architect's estimates of the time required for construction realistic?

11. Did the architect adequately represent the library in negotiations with civil and municipal authorities?

12. Did the architect adequately represent the library in dealings with the contractor?

13. Was the architect easy to work with? Did the architect give due attention to your needs?

14. Was the total of the professional fees paid to the architect consistent with what you were led to expect?

15. Do you feel that you received good value for the money you spent for professional services?

16. Is the building, considering necessary compromises, what you wanted?

17. Would you use this architect again?

When interviewing the architect's references, ask how long ago the services were provided to the references. If any are more than five years old, ask the architect if the same personnel who provided the original services still work in the architect's office. Some offices have a relatively high turnover rate and may bear little resemblance to what they were five or ten years ago.

Decide on a Format for the Interviews

Deciding on a format for the interviews should be relatively straightforward. Interviews should be kept short, simple, and to the point. If possible, schedule all of the interviews for a single day or evening to allow you to make meaningful comparisons among the candidates. Choose the order of the interviews at random. Architects almost never want to be the first interviewed. Selection committees learn how to interview as they go, and subsequent interviews often reveal questions they wished they had asked in the initial interview. A sample format might contain the following:

SET-UP TIME (10 MINUTES). Try to keep ten minutes or so free between the interviews to allow the architects to set up their equipment. Computers may need to be started, projectors fired up, and cables untangled. To expedite the process, ask the architects ahead of time if they require any special facilities for their presentations, and have everything ready to go before the interviews so you won't spend valuable time searching for projection screens or extension cords. If you have a separate room at your disposal, the selection committee could adjourn to discuss a previous interview while the next architect is setting up.

INTRODUCTIONS (5 MINUTES). Introduce the members of the selection committee and ask the architect to briefly introduce team members. The entire design team may not be represented at the interview, but it is important that the person the architect proposes to use as the project manager for your project be there. When scheduling the interview, make sure to tell the architect to bring the project manager. It is important that you meet the project manager, since this person would be your primary contact with the architect.

ARCHITECT'S PRESENTATION (30 MINUTES). Allow architects a predefined amount of time to present whatever they think is appropriate. To keep things fair, designate someone to watch the clock and keep the time limit. You will get a wide variety of presentations, depending on the size and resources of the firms represented. One firm may show a PowerPoint presentation of previous work; another may show renderings; and another may try to dazzle you with a computer-generated walkthrough of their conception of your building.

Try not to be too swayed by impressive presentation styles. A small firm that does high-quality work may not have the resources to dedicate the time required to put together a computerized tour of a proposed building. Your task is to look at the message, not the medium.

QUESTIONS FROM THE COMMITTEE (25–35 MINUTES). Develop a standard set of questions to be put to each architect. Other questions may come up during the interview as a result of the architect's responses, but make sure to cover the entire list of predetermined questions. Some of the questions may be the same ones on the RFQ, and others may be for an oral interview only. You can send the architects the list of questions beforehand. It's up to you, but keep in mind that this is not a contest to determine who is best at "thinking on their feet." You are looking for quality rather than for quickness.

Deciding what to ask the architect during the questions segment of the interview can be difficult. Start by scanning your RFQ for any questions that need elaboration and include them in your script. Here are some suggestions for additional material you might want to cover:

1. What is the architect's in-house organization?

2. Who will be the point of contact with the library?

3. Does the architect have a design philosophy? If so, how would differences of "philosophical" opinion between architect and client be resolved?

4. How does the architect plan to approach this project?

5. What does the architect think is particularly interesting about this project?

6. What are the principal challenges and opportunities?

7. Does the architect plan to involve the public in the design process? If so, how?

8. What services can the architect offer to support passage of a referendum? This is a legitimate question to ask your architect. Be careful, though, not to get involved in a bidding war to see who will offer the most "free" services. Few services are "free." You generally pay the bill somewhere else—usually with a higher architectural fee or a reduced scope of services.

9. If cost overruns or schedule problems on previous projects were apparent during your interviews with the architect's references, give the architect a chance to explain why.

10. How does the architect's firm establish its fees? Don't get into the numbers yet, just find out the architect's standard method for arriving at a fee. Ask how fee adjustments are handled if there are significant change orders or if construction bids come in dramatically higher or lower than the architect estimated.

11. Ask what it is about the architect's firm that makes it the most qualified to do the work.

ADDITIONAL QUESTIONS FROM THE COMMITTEE (10–20 MINUTES). Use this time to ask any additional questions that were inspired by the architect's presentation or answers to your preestablished questions.

COMMITTEE DISCUSSION. Take a few minutes after the interview to sum up your impressions of the architect's presentation and responses. Make careful notes for later review.

And On with the Show

With your list of questions and format for the interviews completed, you are ready to begin the interviews. Include some break time during the interview process so the selection committee members can stretch their legs or have a bite to eat. As an architect, nothing is more disheartening than to arrive at an interview and see the glazed looks of committee members who have just interviewed two or three other firms and are sneaking glances at their watches before you've even begun.

Keep orderly notes of the proceedings and jot down additional comments that occur to you during the committee discussions between interviews. Clients sometimes make audio- or videotapes of the interviews to aid them in later discussions and evaluations. This is permissible as long as the applicants are advised beforehand that the proceedings are being taped. Recording the session is not a substitute for note taking. My own experience is that a well-written set of notes usually offers a better summary of what transpired than an hour's worth of videotape.

Step 6. Select the Architect

What Are You Looking For?

When it comes time to make your selection, the first thing your committee must do is identify the most important qualities you want in an architect. Some of the desired qualities may become apparent only after the interview, related to factors such as these:

1. Quality of the architect's designs
2. Architect's experience in designing buildings of a similar size and use
3. Responses of the architect's references
4. Impressions of the architect's work on previous projects
5. Size of the architect's office in light of the size of your project
6. "Chemistry" among the players and your comfort level with the principal of the firm and the project manager
7. Architect's understanding of your situation and needs
8. Architect's value to the library in nondesign areas, such as political connections or the ability to support a referendum.

The kind of architectural firm you want to do your work is another consideration. Different design firms have different strengths. David Maister, a former professor at the Harvard Business School, defined several generic types of professional firm in *Managing the Professional Service Firm*. His categories offer insight into the ways firms operate and give you an additional way to compare architects. Examining firms in this way can also help you identify traits you wish to have in your architect.

BRAINS (EXPERTISE) FIRMS. These firms are the high-design, high-profile, high-price establishments whose names get a lot of press. They begin their projects with a strong concept and express it throughout the design. The firm you are looking at might not have designed a lot of libraries, but it is accustomed to tackling new building types. If you want a building with real pizzazz, this is your firm. Pizzazz, however, can cut both ways. A strong design concept might feature in the architecture magazines, but it may or may not make a good library. Ask previous clients if this architect's desire to produce award-winning architecture resulted in significant compromises in the functioning of their buildings. If your project is referendum driven, you must also determine if "big design" is appropriate within the political context.

GRAY HAIR (EXPERIENCE) FIRMS. A "gray hair" firm might be characterized as one that has designed numerous libraries and developed a formula that brings a successful result time after time. You would not have to spend much time teaching this kind of firm how a library works. On the other hand, you may get a library design that is somewhat "off the shelf" and simply modified to fit your needs.

PROCEDURE (EXECUTION) FIRMS. This is a "nuts and bolts" outfit. These firms specialize in turning out buildings. They are quick, efficient, relatively inexpensive, and generally not as design oriented. If your building absolutely, positively must go out to bid in six months, this may be the kind of firm to select.

An architectural firm does not usually fall entirely within one of these categories. It can be interesting to ask architects where their firms fall in this group. They may have to express the answer in terms of percentages of each category, such as "50 percent experience and 50 percent execution." Having architects describe their practices in this way can give you insights into how they feel about their businesses, and how they go about serving their clients.

Qualifications-Based Selection

When the interviews are complete, it's time to make your initial selection. The method I describe here is called *qualifications-based selection,* or QBS. The first step in QBS is to assign point values that express how each architect satisfies each of the group's chosen criteria. The list of criteria could be drawn from the list of interview questions above as well as questions asked of the architect's references. Each member of the selection committee individually ranks each architect in each category.

In this system, you might give architect #1 four points out of five for the quality of her designs, five points out of five for the responses of her references, two out of five for her previous experience in library work, and so on for each criterion. Afterward, you total up the point values for each architect and rank the architects from most desired to least desired according to their cumulative scores. The advantage of this scoring system is that it takes some of the subjectivity out of the process. An architect with a score of 50 is definitely more highly rated than one with a score of 45.

So far it's been (relatively) simple—you've figured out which architect the committee likes best. Now is when QBS differs from more traditional methods of selecting professional services. Many states have adopted one form or another of QBS. QBS typically regulates the selection and procurement by public bodies of architectural, engineering, and land surveying firms. The QBS language used by most states is derived from federal legislation, Public Law 92-582, otherwise known as the Brooks Act. The exact language used in your state, if it has adopted QBS, will have to be reviewed by your library's attorney. Because the method described in the Brooks Act is thorough and systematic, I would propose that your library adopt QBS procedures for hiring architects and engineers even if your state does not require you to do so.

In most states, QBS requires you to take many of the steps we have already discussed: advertising for firms, accepting proposals, generating a short list of at least three firms, interviewing firms, and negotiating with the architects. But one important feature isn't on this list, and this facet of QBS is what makes it unique.

Until now, fees for professional services have been noticeably absent from our discussions. The true purpose of QBS is to ensure that professionals hired to do work for public bodies are selected primarily on the basis of their qualifications and only secondarily by their fees. Using the QBS method, the public body begins contract negotiations with the top-rated architect. Indeed, discussing fees is prohibited during the initial selection process. If a price for services is agreed on, that's the end of the procedure. You can sign the contract and begin the project. If you cannot settle on a price, you can then begin contract negotiations with the architect with the next highest rating. Here's the rub: Once you move on to the second architect, you cannot resume negotiations with the first. If you cannot settle with the second architect, you have to go on to the third and are prohibited from resuming negotiations with either of the first two. This process continues until you settle on a fee with an architect or run out of applicants. If you run out, you have to begin the entire process again, beginning by advertising another RFQ. That is a powerful incentive to settle on a fee with someone in the first group of candidates.

You Get What You Pay For

I warned you that we would eventually come back to this topic. It could equally be said that you seldom get what you don't pay for. As you may have realized from the above discussion, the intent of the Brooks Act is to ensure that public agencies select according to quality rather than by price alone. The Brooks Act prevents public agencies from using one architect's fee as a lever to bargain down the fee of another. This legislation's authors recognized that, when you bargain down a fee, you are also likely to be bargaining away some of the services you would otherwise receive. For public work, it was judged that the overall quality and completeness of the work were more important to the public safety than the apparent savings of a relatively small amount in professional fees.

If you are accountable for spending the public's money, you no doubt understand a dilemma inherent in hiring a professional. You want high-quality work, but in these tight times how can you explain to the taxpayers that you didn't hire the lowest "bidder." You realize that you might be leaving yourself open to charges of favoritism or other irregularities. With QBS, the architect's qualifications rather than the architect's fees become the basis of the "bids," and all negotiations follow a set procedure. If the fees seem excessive, you can always move on to another candidate. Thus, competitive pressures are still brought to bear on the architects as they state their fees.

A Question of Self-Interest

Public servants have to protect themselves from incurring liability. Whether you choose to follow a QBS process or something else, it is incumbent on you to make sure your selection will promote the public's welfare. If the library fails to select an architect or engineer for a project without basing the selection on qualifications, and there is a collapse or other failure that results in injury or death, the board could be found negligent. Selection established by price alone may not be in either the taxpayers' or your own best interests.

Not long ago I attended a seminar for architects given by an attorney. The question of fee shopping for professional services came up. The attorney asked if, legalities aside, we would take bids to have our wisdom teeth extracted. If we were to do so, would we really want to use the low bidder? This is not really such a bad parallel. You could almost always find someone to provide architectural services for less money. Where do you draw the line? What if one architect is much less expensive than the others but has done only sunroom additions for residential clients; would you really want that firm to design your new library? QBS is intended to circumvent this kind of dilemma.

Step 7. Negotiate with the Architect

The interviews are completed, and the architects have been rated according to the selection committee's preferences and informed of the results. You are ready to sit down and hammer out a deal for the professional services with the top-rated firm.

Where do you start? Before you begin, it may pay to do some homework regarding the different ways architects can deliver their services and try to formulate some ideas regarding which method best suits your needs. Because most publicly owned organizations follow the traditional design/bid/build approach, I emphasize that method here, though also touching on the alternatives, for those organizations able to use them. See chapter 12 for descriptions of the most common forms of project delivery.

Across the Table

Once you decide which services you think you'll need from your architect and have an idea of the best way those services should be presented, you are ready to sit down and begin working out the details of a client/architect agreement.

The architect often proposes using one of the standard AIA agreements. There are several different AIA contracts from which to choose. The appropriate contract depends on your particular circumstances. Beyond the "Standard Form of Agreement between Owner and Architect" (Contract B141), there are specialized contracts for designated services, interior design services, projects of limited scope, services performed when the client is using a construction manager, and others. The chances are that the architect will propose using B141 as the basis of your agreement, and I assume the use of B141 in this discussion.

Unless you have a pressing reason to do otherwise, I suggest that you stick to standard AIA contracts. Although they were written on behalf of architects, they do a reasonably good job at maintaining impartiality with respect to both the architect and the client. These standard contracts have been developed over many years and cover most of the issues that are likely to come up between client and architect. Some large corporations and public bodies have their own custom contracts. I advise that you steer away from writing your own unless your attorney has particular experience in this field and a good background in construction law. As with all contracts, your attorney should review the one the architect presents to the library. At this time, the attorney can suggest additions or alterations to the standard language that seem to be in the best interest of the library.

The first step in the process is to sit down with the architect for a general discussion of the project and your expectations of what services you need. The list of required services you generated earlier is your starting point. As a part of the discussion, the architect may suggest modifications to your list. A good goal for this first meeting is to arrive at an agreement with the architect concerning the scope of services to be provided. Direct the architect to prepare a proposal for services and a draft contract for review by the library's board, director, and attorney. Ask the architect to send you this material before the next meeting so you have time to review it and formulate your questions. If the architect desires, the fee portion could be left blank until it can be discussed at the next meeting. If the negotiations are being undertaken by a construction committee, be sure that the material is reviewed and approved by the entire board before proceeding.

Before You Sign on the Dotted Line

Before the next meeting with the architect, photocopy the architect's proposal and preliminary contract so everyone has a copy. The library director and perhaps a board member should read through all of this, line by line. It can be a lengthy

Nothing astonishes men so much as common sense and plain dealing.

—Ralph Waldo Emerson

document, so you can expect to be at it for some time. This is an important task. Someone other than the library's attorney should have a thorough understanding of the commitments the library is making by signing the contract, as well as an overview of the range of the architect's responsibilities.

Your attorney may have suggested some changes to the standard contract. Paragraph 1.3.5 mandates arbitration as the means of settling claims or disputes relating to the architectural agreement. This section is often deleted or modified by the library's lawyer. Discuss all proposed alterations to the contract to ensure that everyone is agreed. A single, master copy of the contract could be marked up during the session and then photocopied so everyone has a record of the agreement.

One last item of particular interest is the architect's reimbursable expenses. Postage, phone calls, printing, computer-aided drafting, renderings, and models are among the items discussed here. In addition to agreeing about items to be included as reimbursables, you should discuss what forms of documentation you require from the architect to substantiate claims for reimbursement. Things like expenses for reproductions and long-distance phone calls are relatively easy, since the architect can provide receipts and phone bills as backup. For things like the cost of drawing renderings and building models, you may have to rely on the architect's records of hours spent on the task. Whenever possible, get the architect to agree to a maximum cost for those kinds of service. Because of uncertainty regarding the scope of these additional services, the architect may not be willing to commit to a cost until later in the project, when the scope is better defined.

The Bottom Line

The last step in negotiating with your architect is agreeing on a fee. There are several ways an architect can put together a fee for the project. Here are the most common arrangements:

FEE AS A STIPULATED SUM. In this arrangement, architects set the fee on the basis of their determination of the value of the services to be provided, which are often calculated from estimates of the number of hours and other expenses required to complete the project. An advantage of this method is that the client and architect know what the fees are before the project begins. Should the scope of the project increase after the contract is signed, the architect's fee can be adjusted upward in proportion to the change. When another method is used to determine the architect's fee for basic services, stipulated sums are often used to define costs for any additional services.

FEE AS A PERCENTAGE OF THE CONSTRUCTION COST. This is probably the most common arrangement. It assumes that the larger the project, the more time it takes the architect to design, draw, and coordinate the project. This assumption that difficulty parallels project size is sometimes borne out, sometimes not. With this method, the final fee cannot be calculated until the project is bid and built. Therefore, early payments to the architect are based on the estimated cost of the project, with adjustments made later as the cost of the project is determined. Exactly what is included in the "construction cost" must be clearly defined beforehand.

COST-PLUS FEE. This type of fee is based on the direct costs to the architect plus one sort of addition or another. There are several variations:

1. Multiple of the architect's direct salary expenses. This is a multiple of the architect's payroll.

2. Multiple of the architect's direct personnel expense. This is like the above but includes the fringe benefits of the staff in the equation.

3. Professional fee plus expenses. This begins with a "professional fee," to which the architect's expenses are added. The professional fee is a figure negotiated between the architect and the client.

4. Hourly. This is usually based on a predetermined billing rate for each employee. The rates should be agreed on before the contract is signed.

The major disadvantage of cost-plus fee arrangements is that the client may not have any idea of the eventual total. If you are considering this type of arrangement, I recommend that you ask the architect to give you a "cost not to exceed" figure that fixes the maximum amount the library could be billed.

Cost-plus fees are most suited to projects of limited duration for which the scope of the work has not been fully established, and they are often used for initial feasibility studies. They are sometimes prohibited for publicly funded projects because of the uncertainty of the magnitude of the fee.

How Much?

Each project has its own set of circumstances that influence the amount of the architect's fee. There are some general rules that apply to most projects. One is that the fee should reflect the difficulty of the project. Looked at as a percentage of the project cost, the architect's fee for designing a warehouse would be relatively less than the fee for designing a hospital or library. Similarly, building additions are often charged at a higher percentage than new construction because of the increased complexity of working with existing construction. A second general rule is that fees are proportionately higher for smaller projects. The fee an architect would have to charge to design and bid a new circulation desk for a library would probably be a much higher percentage of the project cost than the fee for designing an entire new library. The circulation desk would, of course, be a much smaller project with perhaps only one sheet of details compared to dozens of architectural sheets for an entire building. Similarly, the percentage fee for designing a 70,000-square-foot library would usually be less than the percentage for designing a similar library of 20,000 square feet. Another general rule is that projects with special requirements, like abbreviated or lengthy schedules, generally cost more, since the architect must make up for overtime pay in the first case or, in the second case, for the greater number of hours expended.

It is difficult to generalize about what percentage fees ought to be. To illustrate the point, the State of Illinois used to publish a table detailing how it would pay architects for state-sponsored construction projects. It was based on a sliding scale; the fee for a $300,000 building addition might be 14 percent of the cost of construction, while a fee for a new $300 million building project might be 3.5 percent of the cost of construction.

Sticker Shock

In the discussion on construction documents (chapter 7), I gave some examples of the time it takes an architect to produce a set of working drawings. Some offices assume 40–60 hours on each sheet of drawings. On this assumption, a small project of twelve or so architectural sheets requires 480–720 hours of drawing time.

Multiply these hours by the billing rate for the architect's staff, which may be somewhere between $100 and $200 per hour, and you wind up with some significant costs—and these are just the architect's portion of the fee. The fees for engineers and other consultants have to be added. On top of this, consider that time spent by the project managers or principals is usually billed at a higher rate, and that the construction documents portion of the project may be only something like 40 percent of the architect's total fee.

Unless you are accustomed to dealing with fees for professional services, such figures can be surprising. More than once, I've seen client jaws drop when they heard the proposed fee for a project. Things usually settle down when we explain how we arrive at the fee, but there can be a few uncomfortable moments for everyone until the explanation is understood.

As one of the people responsible for selecting the architect, you may have to deal with such "sticker shock." You may at first be alarmed by the fee. You began the negotiation process with the firm you want to do the work. Do you accept this fee or move on to another architect? An alternative to moving on to the next architect is to negotiate with the first architect for a lower fee. Sometimes the architect will have started with a "rock bottom" fee and be unwilling to go any lower; at other times there may be some room for negotiation.

There is nothing wrong with asking an architect for some backup information to show how a fee was established. Sometimes this is less an issue of affordability than one of you being able to justify the expense to the taxpayers or whoever else is in control of the project funding. In this case, the backup information supplied by the architect can give you some of the justification you need. Going back to your discussions with the architect's references is another approach. If most of them feel they received good value for the money spent on professional fees, you have an added reason for negotiating with this architect rather than going on to your second choice.

In the final analysis, you have to satisfy yourself that you have arrived at an equitable fee arrangement. When the board is comfortable with the amount, you can sit down and sign the contract. Hiring an architect can take a surprising amount of your time. If you give it the attention it deserves and use some of the methods outlined in this chapter, chances are that you will have no reason to regret your decision.

Project Delivery

There are several basic ways a building project can be designed, bid, and built. In this chapter we look at some of the most common methods of project delivery. Each method has its own demands on the client and its own benefits and drawbacks. I focus on methods that are most suitable for small to mid-size libraries and also on those that require the least in-house expertise and least time spent by library staff and trustees.

Most of the following methods of project delivery can be better understood by looking at them in terms of contracts. In coming to understand "who is working for whom," you develop a better appreciation of each player's project responsibilities.

Traditional Design-Bid-Build Project Delivery

Design-bid-build is the most commonly used form of project delivery. It is accepted by all states and in some places is required for public work. In a design-bid-build project the client has separate contracts with the architect and the builder. The contractual arrangement is represented in figure 12-1, in which solid lines indicate contractual relationships and dotted lines indicate the flow of information among elements of the project team.

One of the characteristics of the design-bid-build process is its defined, linear sequence. The architect is hired initially to produce a set of documents that enables the project to be bid. A builder is then selected and hired based on the results of the bidding. After the project is bid and the contract is let, the architect functions as the client's representative, administering the construction contract and helping to ensure that the contractor's work is in accordance with the drawings and specifications.

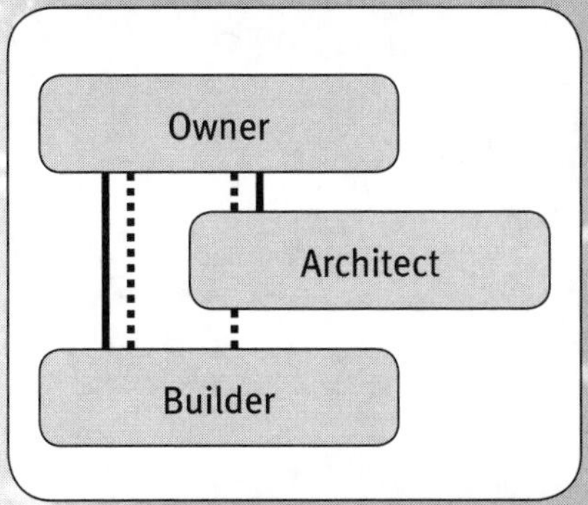

ADVANTAGES OF DESIGN-BID-BUILD PROJECT DELIVERY

- The client is intimately involved in the decisions made during the design and programming phases. (The nature of your involvement in that process is the subject of the previous chapters in this book.)

- Your building is completely designed before it goes to bid. There is a full set of plans and specifications that shows exactly what you should be getting. The architect's periodic price estimates should give you a good idea of the eventual cost of your project.

- The architect is working for you, not for the contractor, and so can be expected to look after your best interests.

- Competitive bidding helps keep the overall project cost to a minimum.

- Design-bid-build is the most widely used project delivery method. Most contractors, suppliers, and clients are familiar with its basic principles.

> *The intellect of man is forced to choose: Perfection of the life, or of the work.*
> —W. B. Yeats

> *You pays your money and you takes your chances.*
> —Punch

Figure 12-1

DISADVANTAGES OF DESIGN-BID-BUILD PROJECT DELIVERY

- The price for the building is not determined until the project is bid. Interest rate fluctuations and contractor workloads can have a significant impact on the final price. These factors may be impossible to predict and can cause the price to deviate from the architect's estimates.

- Design-bid-build is organized into three distinct, sequential phases. Each phase must be completed before the next can begin, and so the total project duration may be longer than with some other project delivery methods. (Project duration for a mid-size library usually runs 22–26 months from the time you sign the architect's contract until you move into your new building.)

- You do not know who your contractor is until the bids are opened and the lowest qualified bidder is identified. For a publicly funded project, it may be difficult to reject a low bidder whom you regard as unqualified or otherwise unsuitable.

Construction Management

There are many different forms of "construction management," and the term is often misunderstood. If you are considering utilizing a construction-management approach, it is important that you understand its ramifications.

When speaking with clients, I have often heard the term "construction management" confused with "construction observation." Construction management usually means that a new entity—the construction manager—is hired by the client to fulfill one of several roles. By contrast, construction observation comprises the architect's many visits to the job site to observe the work and verify that it is in general conformance with the specifications. Construction observation is one of an architect's traditional services and part of each of the project delivery options we explore in this chapter.

Before we look at some of the different forms of construction management, I offer this warning. Unlike architects, construction managers are not always licensed or regulated by the state. When that is the case, anyone can advertise themselves as a construction manager. Although construction management can be the right choice for many projects, "construction mismanagement" is not unknown. Because of the lack of regulation and the many different forms construction management can assume, the interview and selection process you use to select your construction manager is doubly important. Place special emphasis on references from both architects and clients and don't allow yourself to be swayed by slick presentations. It can be a good idea to involve your architect in the construction management selection process.

Construction Manager as Builder (At-Risk Construction Management)

This is one of the most common forms of construction management. In this arrangement, a construction manager divides a project into several "bid packages," each of which is put out for bid. The low bidder for each bid package becomes the prime contractor for the work described in that bid package. Often the bid packages are organized by trade. If so, there may be a prime contractor for electrical work, another for plumbing, another for ventilation, and so on. So far, this sounds pretty much like what a general contractor does after bidding a project, but there are several important differences. The contractual arrangement for this form of construction management is symbolized in figure 12-2, again with contractual relationships indicated by solid lines and the flow of information by dashed lines.

In this version of construction management, the construction manager assumes the role and responsibility of a general contractor, and thus also the potential risks and liabilities inherent in general contracting, since he holds the contracts with the prime contractors.

The potential benefits to the client are primarily those of cost and scheduling. Let's look at the cost aspect first. Because the construction manager takes multiple competitive bids for each trade, the overall cost might be lower than if a single contractor was submitting a bid for the entire project. The idea is that competitive pressure from each of these separate bids results in lower prices than would be possible if the project were bid as a whole from a single general contractor. For example, in putting together a bid for a building, a general contractor may get prices from one or two drywall subcontractors whom the general contractor has worked with in the past. The construction manager, on the other hand, might elect to put out a "drywall package" that might solicit prices from fifteen or twenty drywall contractors. In other words, the construction manager is getting prices from a much wider range of contractors than would a general contractor, and a greater number of bidders will likely result in lower prices.

The construction manager charges the client for the time spent coordinating all these bids, so the construction management fees must be deducted before calculating any potential savings. Since bids are not taken both on a general contractor basis and from a construction manager, it can never be known how much money, if any, a client has been saved by construction management.

Sometimes the construction manager gives the client a bid and begins construction before the architect has fully completed the drawings. This is known as *fast-track construction*. Usually fast-track construction takes the form of getting an early start on foundations or ordering items that require long lead time, like steel, to minimize construction time. If your schedule is particularly tight and you want to go this route, it is important that the architect be aware of it, since the construction documents must be specially formatted to enable the construction manager to go out for early bids. We look at some of the risks and benefits of fast-track construction later in this chapter.

Another service construction managers can provide before the bids are taken is known as *value engineering*. In value engineering, the construction manager performs periodic reviews of the architect's construction documents and advises the client and architect of changes that could help keep the overall estimated project costs within the budget. This process takes place to some degree on every project that doesn't have a limitless budget, whether or not a construction manager is involved. As architects, we are always looking for a less expensive way to achieve our design goals. Having a third party (the construction manager) advise the architect on where to cut back offers the benefit of another pair of eyes looking out for the client but also can cause friction within the project team—particularly if the architect believes the suggested changes might compromise the architectural integrity of the building.

One advantage of at-risk construction management project delivery is that for the client there is a single source of responsibility for construction. As with a

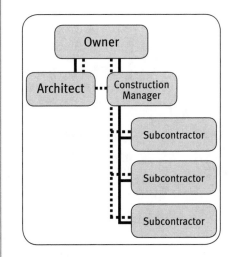

Figure 12-2

traditional general contractor arrangement, the construction manager holds the contracts with the prime contractors and thus is solely responsible for the performance and quality of their work. This insulates the client from many of the inevitable headaches that can be part of building a new library.

ADVANTAGES OF AT-RISK CONSTRUCTION MANAGEMENT

- The client has a choice in the selection of the builder, rather than the selection being based solely on the low bidder.
- The client can get an early commitment to a building cost (see "Guaranteed Maximum Price," below).
- Construction time can be shorter than for conventional design-bid-build projects (see "Fast-track Construction," below)
- After a construction management firm is selected, the construction manager can work with and advise the architect while the drawings are being completed. This can result in a more "buildable" project and help circumvent later difficulties.
- The construction manager may have more in-house expertise relating to cost control than does the architect. This can help keep building costs in line.
- The construction manager offers the client single-source responsibility for construction-related issues.
- In most instances the architect is working for you, not for the contractor, and so can be expected to look after your best interests.

DISADVANTAGES OF AT-RISK CONSTRUCTION MANAGEMENT

- The construction manager is another entity inserted into the construction process. There is no guarantee that project cost savings will make up for the construction manager's fees.
- In the case of fast-track construction, the chances for contractor's claims for "extras" because of changes of project scope are increased when the construction manager's bids are based on partially completed drawings.
- Disputes between architects and construction managers are possible, usually over extra costs or construction quality. The client has separate contracts with the architect and construction manager and can wind up in the middle of these disputes.
- In conventional bidding, general contractors often have a stable of subcontractors who are known entities and with whom they often work. The many separate bid packages put out by the construction manager can result in the construction management hiring low-bidding subcontractors that may be new to the construction manager; this could cause quality and performance problems.

Construction Manager as Advisor

This version of construction management lies somewhere between traditional design-bid-build and construction manager as builder. In this project delivery option, a construction manager is hired and made a part of the team, preferably during the design phase of the project. As in traditional design-bid-build, the client, not the construction manager, holds the contracts with the builder. The construction manager's function is limited to advising the client, with responsibilities varying from project to project depending on the client's needs. This option is most often used by clients who want increased control over a building project but do not have the time or staff resources to dedicate to it. In this case clients primarily want to hire someone to represent their interests. Figure 12-3 suggests the contractual relationships and lines of communication in this approach.

In its simplest form, this delivery option could use the construction manager as a client's representative who attends project meetings, monitors contractor's requests for payment, performs limited site observations, and makes periodic reports to the client. On the other end of the spectrum, the construction manager could be contracted early to represent the client while the architect is completing the building design and preparing the construction documents. In one version of this delivery option, the construction manager divides the project into several smaller bid packages and oversees the bidding of each bid package. But, unlike the construction management-as-builder option, here the client holds the contracts with each of the subcontractors. The advantages of price savings from the many bid packages would be somewhat offset by the construction manager's fee as well as the increased liability the client incurs by directly holding many smaller contracts. Although the client may be holding these contracts, it is part of the construction manager's job to coordinate the contracts and relieve the client of the day-to-day responsibilities of running the project. A good construction manager insulates the client from most construction phase headaches.

In any construction manager-as-advisor scenario, it is important that the client pay special attention to the roles of the construction manager and architect. Because these roles overlap to some degree, there is the possibility of paying twice for some services and well as an increased chance for confusion and disputes. Because of this, each player's responsibilities should be determined before the construction manager is retained. Your architect may also be able to assist you with the construction management selection process.

ADVANTAGES OF CONSTRUCTION MANAGER AS ADVISOR

- The selection of the construction manager can be based on qualifications, not low bid. This is particularly suitable for very large or complex projects.
- The client is relieved of many of the day-to-day tasks that arise during the design and construction of a new building.
- The construction manager can provide expertise for clients who have little or no experience in administering a construction project.
- The construction manager provides a second set of eyes to assist the architect in monitoring the quality of documents and construction. This can reduce the number of change orders.
- The appropriate construction manager can enable the client to fast-track the project.

DISADVANTAGES OF CONSTRUCTION MANAGER AS ADVISOR

- Another player is inserted into the construction process. This adds an additional level of complexity into an already complicated process.

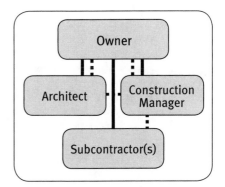

Figure 12-3

- Project cost or time savings may not make up for the construction manager's fees.

- Limits of authority between construction managers and architects can be difficult to define, leading to conflicts within the project team and a diffusion of responsibility.

- Because the client directly holds each subcontractor's contract, there is an increase in potential liability.

- Projects increase in complexity as the construction manager subdivides the project into separately bid prime contracts.

- The client is less insulated from scheduling problems or conflicts between subcontractors than is the case when a general contractor or construction manager is holding the contracts.

Design-Build

One form of project delivery—design-build—combines contractor and architect in a single entity. In the most widely used form, the design-build firm carries the responsibility for both the design and construction phases of the project, as suggested in figure 12-4. One of the chief advantages of design-build is that it can reduce the time required to complete a building, in part because there is no traditional bidding phase. Another advantage is that the design-build contractors often offer a guaranteed maximum price relatively early in the process.

Before hiring a design-builder, many clients begin by retaining an architect to do the program analysis and afterward to take the project into the schematic design phase (see chapters 4 and 6). In this way, a building design is produced that is detailed enough for potential design-builders to use for their estimating. These estimates form the basis of competitive bids, which for public work usually award the project to the lowest qualified design-build bidder. After the project is awarded, the design-build firm may use its own staff to complete the construction documents.

The typical design-build firm has both architects and contractors on staff who work together to produce your building. Alternately, the design-build entity may be an association between independent architects and builders. The primary advantage to you is that under this system the design-build firm is a single source of responsibility.

There are several shortcomings inherent in the design-build process. During the construction phase of a conventional (design-bid-build) project, the architect is working directly for the client, representing the client's interests. With the design-build system, the architect works for the design-build company, not for the client. This carries the risk that, in a dispute between a contractor and the client, the concerns of the client might not be adequately represented.

When a guaranteed maximum price (see below) has been offered, the design-build firm is vested with the responsibility of bringing in the project on time and within budget. That sounds good, but the other side of the equation is that the design-build firm has the ability, to a degree, to make changes in the project to ensure that the time and budget criteria are met. This can tend to reduce the client's input in the decision-making process and opens up the possibility of quality being sacrificed to stay within budget.

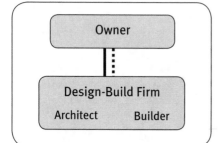

Figure 12-4

Because of the potential for conflicts of interest, the AIA for many years prohibited architects from participating in design-build arrangements. The prohibition was reconsidered in 1978, and design-build was incorporated into the AIA's revised code of ethics in 1987.

Many states require that public work use separate contracts for design and construction. This follows, in part, from laws that require competitive bids for work of any significant size. You should always consult legal counsel if you are considering using a design-build form of project delivery.

ADVANTAGES OF DESIGN-BUILD PROJECT DELIVERY

- The client has a single source of responsibility for design and construction.
- The elimination of the traditional bidding process can reduce overall project duration.
- The client is insulated from potential conflicts between designers and builders, since these are resolved within the design-build firm.
- Guaranteed maximum prices can be generated relatively early in the design process.

DISADVANTAGES OF DESIGN-BUILD PROJECT DELIVERY

- In some places, design-build is not permitted for public work.
- The architect works for the design-build company rather than directly for the client. This can eliminate an important "check and balance" that is part of a traditionally bid project, in which the architect works for the client and is responsible for verifying the contractor's adherence to the contract documents.
- The combination of the lack of an independent architect and a design-build firm that was selected on a low-bid basis can diminish the quality of the project.
- Selecting design-build firms can be difficult without extensive preparation. Much up-front effort is required to provide adequate definition of the proposed building before a meaningful comparison of design-builders' proposals is possible. Clients without construction experience may have difficulty assembling an appropriate package of information.
- Because so much of a design-build project is performed within the design-build firm, the client's participation in the process is lessened. This represents a savings of the client's time, but it makes it more difficult for the client to stay in touch with the project.
- The client gives up a degree of control when projects are bid on a guaranteed maximum price. When combined with the client's reduced role in the design-build process, this can lead to misunderstandings regarding the scope of the project and what was included in the designer-builder's bid.

Fast-Track Construction: Building in the Fast Lane

There are risks inherent in fast-tracking, and two primary reasons that some clients elect to run these risks and use this form of project scheduling. One reason is that the project price is known (and sometimes guaranteed by the construction manager) relatively early in the process. The other is that construction can begin quickly. The construction manager can bid your project and begin building the foundations and ordering long lead-time items like structural steel (assuming those portions of the architectural drawings are complete) while the architect is still drawing the rest of the building. In theory, this could enable construction to begin months earlier than it otherwise would. This can be an important benefit if you absolutely must meet a specific deadline for moving into your new building. For this reason, fast-tracking is often used for educational buildings that must be ready to occupy when school opens.

If your project has unusual time constraints, say a requirement to vacate your existing building by a certain date, it may be necessary to take measures to expedite the construction process. The design of the entire building might be taken as far as the design development phase, at which time the architect focuses on the parts of the project that happen first during construction; thus, the architect would turn out detailed foundation and structural drawings and specifications before refining the rest of the design. As construction work begins on the foundations and the steel is ordered, the architect completes the rest of the building design.

Potholes

You can probably imagine why the fast-track method entails risks. First, because the building design isn't complete yet, you or your construction manager do not have a finished set of construction documents from which to estimate final costs when construction begins. You also lose some flexibility. Many design decisions are made earlier in the process than would otherwise be the case, and changes to the design become increasingly impractical as the foundations already in the ground begin to fix the size and configuration of the building. If it turns out that previously poured foundations do have to be removed and relocated for subsequent design changes, you lose the time advantage of the fast-track method in addition to paying twice for the foundations. For fast-track projects, it is a good idea to set aside a larger contingency to cover these eventualities. A fast-tracked project nearly always costs more than the same project built on a traditional design-bid-build basis.

Fast-tracking also depends on a high degree of coordination, cooperation, and expertise on the part of the construction manager, contractors, architect, and client. Such projects require experienced management to be brought off successfully. As a general rule, you should consider other options available to you before deciding on fast-track construction.

Guaranteed Maximum Price

Construction managers often offer clients a guaranteed maximum price relatively early in the process. This price is based on partially completed construction documents, often at the end of the schematic design phase. The concept of a guaranteed maximum price early in the project can be attractive to a client, especially when planning project budgets or fund-raising. However, putting together such a price requires the construction manager to make many assumptions regarding the portions of the documents that have yet to be completed. The price is usually contingent on what the estimator has assumed as the complete scope of the project. If the architect or client subsequently adds something to the project, the construction manager can make the case that this is not covered by the guaranteed maximum price and declare it an extra cost, necessitating a change order to increase the budget to accommodate this change of scope.

In the effort to avoid additional costs, there can be many heated discussions involving the client, architect, and construction manager regarding what does and does not count as a change of scope. Sometimes the construction manager's argument for extra money for a change of scope is legitimate, and the cost of the building increases. This happens often enough that the concept of a "guaranteed maximum price" should always be taken with a grain of salt, especially when it is combined with fast-track construction.

In some guaranteed-maximum-price projects, the contractor is empowered to make changes in the building design to hold the cost to the guaranteed maximum. This can result in something of a shell game in which the construction manager makes reductions in one part of a project to cover extra costs elsewhere. In trying to maintain a guaranteed maximum price, the construction manager can be tempted to save money on the less visible parts of your building. This is sometimes done by lowering the quality of things like mechanical systems and door hardware. Savings on systems such as these may be only short-term savings that quickly lose their value as their maintenance costs begin to add up in a few years. At these times, the importance of the architect's role as your agent is paramount.

The best way to avoid some of the problems we've just discussed is to hire an architect that is independent of the construction manager and to insist on explicit documentation for any changes the construction manager may make. Having the architect and construction manager work together early in the process while the drawings are still underway can help ensure that everyone has the same understanding of the scope of your project. When everyone agrees on the scope of the work, the dilemma of guaranteed maximum price versus guaranteed minimum product need not come up.

Don't Forget Quality-Based Selection

The QBS process for choosing architects (see chapter 11) is equally applicable to the selection of construction managers and design-build firms. Many states require that QBS be used as the basis for selecting architects, engineers, construction managers, and design-build firms for public work.

Summary

In the final analysis, construction management is most applicable to projects that have a higher than normal degree of complexity or tight schedules. Before deciding on a construction management form of project delivery, you should convince yourself that special difficulties associated with your project are enough to offset the potentially significant additional fees associated with hiring a construction manager. Deciding what form of project delivery to use can be a daunting task. Your architect can help you decide which form is most suitable to your situation.

Chapter 13

> *No generation can contract debts greater than may be paid during the course of its own existence.*
>
> —Thomas Jefferson

Sustainable Design

These days, the media seem full of environmental news: melting polar ice caps, shrinking tropical forests, rising levels of carbon dioxide, increasing hurricane activity, vanishing species. Environmental news is everywhere, and most of the news isn't good. In addition to the environmental questions, our dependence on fossil fuels poses ever-increasing risk to our security as we compete for a limited number of natural resources. Our military is in parts of the world that we would be happy to ignore if it weren't for the fact that they sit on top of oil reserves.

Protecting our environment and reducing our dependence on foreign oil are only two of many compelling reasons for reevaluating the ways we live, work—and build. We all make personal choices that determine how large of an environmental footprint we make; turning the thermostat up in the summer or down in the winter, household recycling, driving a compact or hybrid car in place of an SUV. We are faced with similar choices when given the responsibility for constructing a new building or remodeling an existing structure. These decisions can have effects that endure for generations.

In the United States, buildings are responsible for approximately 36 percent of our overall energy usage and more than 65 percent of our electricity consumption. They are responsible for half of the sulfur dioxide emissions and more than a third of overall carbon dioxide emissions. Looking at these statistics, it stands to reason that increasing the sustainability of our buildings can have a significant positive environmental impact.

What Is Sustainability?

The terms "sustainability" and "green design" are used interchangeably. In its broadest sense, sustainability can be defined in terms of one goal: meeting the needs of the current generation without placing a burden on future generations. Thomas Jefferson summed it up well. In both environmental and financial terms, the goal of sustainability is to live within our means.

In terms of the environment, living within one's means can be taken in several different ways. It can imply that a building, during its construction and during its useful lifetime, returns the lowest possible amount of carbon back into the atmosphere. It might mean that the building is constructed with the least amount of energy. It can mean that the design utilizes renewable resources in place of hydrocarbons and that recycled materials are used wherever possible. Appropriate sustainability strategies, such as those shown in figure 13-1, and the suitable level of sustainability vary from project to project.

In addition to being good for our environment, sustainable design can have other benefits for the building's users: increased comfort for the occupants, "healthier" buildings, lower energy costs, and increased productivity. The benefits of green design become clearer when we look at the details of techniques of sustainability.

Measuring Sustainability: LEED

As the need for sustainable design became more apparent, so did the need for an objective way to measure sustainability—something to provide an organized framework for those contemplating sustainable design and to define specific goals for a green building. In the United States, the task of developing this framework fell to the U.S. Green Building Council (USGBC). Improving on sustainable programs in use in Europe, the USGBC developed a program aimed at both quantifying and promoting green design. That program is called LEED (Leadership in Energy and Environmental Design).

The LEED system is point based. More than forty concepts have been defined as sustainable criteria and given LEED credits. Each credit has been assigned a point value; most are worth a single point, and some are worth more.

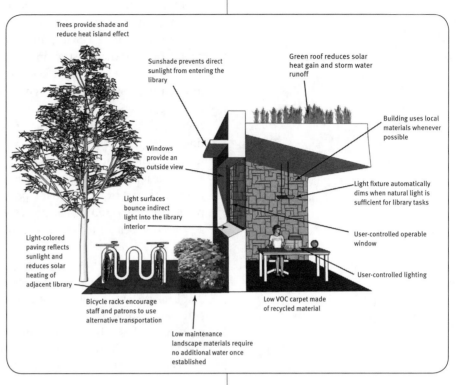

Trees provide shade and reduce heat island effect

Sunshade prevents direct sunlight from entering the library

Green roof reduces solar heat gain and storm water runoff

Building uses local materials whenever possible

Windows provide an outside view

Light surfaces bounce indirect light into the library interior

Light-colored paving reflects sunlight and reduces solar heating of adjacent library

Light fixture automatically dims when natural light is sufficient for library tasks

User-controlled operable window

User-controlled lighting

Bicycle racks encourage staff and patrons to use alternative transportation

Low VOC carpet made of recycled material

Low maintenance landscape materials require no additional water once established

Figure 13-1
Sustainability strategies

If you qualify for a minimum number of credits, your project can become LEED certified. Achieving additional credits moves the project up to different levels of certification. Here are the levels of certification defined to date:

Certified	26–32 points
Silver Level	33–38 points
Gold Level	39–51 points
Platinum Level	52 or more points

The USGBC program also offers training in the LEED system and provides an examination which, if passed, earns the applicant the designation LEED-Accredited Professional.

One of the hallmarks of the LEED system is that it is holistic. It encourages an integrated approach to the entire project, not just the building itself. This becomes clearer when we look at some of the LEED credits and how they work.

To gain LEED certification for your project, you have to do more than say that you have achieved a certain number of points. Documentation is required for every step. For the most part, this information is provided by the design team and submitted to the USGBC. As you might suspect, preparing the documentation required for LEED certification is not covered in a standard architectural contract. The time needed would qualify as an additional service and merit additional professional fees for both the architect and the various engineers employed by the architect who assist in the documentation.

The LEED process begins by registering your project with the USGBC. As the administrator of the program, the USGBC charges a fee for project registration to cover the time involved to evaluate projects. A successful LEED project should have LEED certification as a goal from the very beginning. It is difficult to come in after the fact and try to get a project LEED certified because of the holistic nature of the program. It is possible to apply sustainable criteria to a project without actually registering with the USGBC and save some of the time and money dedicated to paperwork and the registration process. Registration should, however, be pursued for the simple reason that it keeps us honest and provides the incentive to follow through with sustainable design. Some sustainable features don't add cost to a building; others do. As soon as the budget gets tight, there is the temptation to cut back on the sustainability of the project to control costs. Pursuing LEED certification forces the design team to be more creative and search out other sustainable features that might reach the same result at a more palatable cost.

Once a project is registered, the design team begins to assemble the documentation required by LEED. Many project decisions are made in order to qualify for particular LEED credits. The process can have an impact on everything from where a project is located to how it is constructed and how it is used. Let's look at the LEED system and see what impact it might have on your library. Examining the credit system is the best way to get an overview of what LEED is about.

In most of this chapter, we look at a list of the credits utilized in LEED version 2.1. This system is always being refined, and some of these credits will undoubtedly be modified as LEED matures. Most of the credits are voluntary; the design team picks those that are most achievable or applicable to the project. There are also mandatory credits, termed "prerequisites," that must be achieved on every LEED project. The credits are divided into six major groups:

SS	Sustainable Sites
WE	Water Efficiency
EA	Energy and Atmosphere
MR	Materials and Resources
EQ	Environmental Quality
ID	Innovation and Design Process

The following discussion presents a broad and subjective overview of each credit. For more information, see the *LEED Reference Guide* published by the USGBC.

Sustainable Site Credits

SS PREREQUISITE 1. EROSION AND SEDIMENTATION CONTROL (PREREQUISITE; NO POINTS AWARDED)

This credit mandates that erosion control measures must be implemented on building sites to prevent silt from entering waterways. As is the case with all prerequisites, this must be incorporated into all LEED projects. Control often takes the form of silt control fences and reseeding bare soil disturbed by the construction process.

SS CREDIT 1. SITE SELECTION (1 POINT)

Build on appropriate sites that reduce the environmental impact of the project. Essentially, don't build on floodplains, prime farmland, or sites that will have a negative impact on endangered species.

SS CREDIT 2. DEVELOPMENT DENSITY (1 POINT)

Build as close to existing urban areas as possible and utilize existing infrastructure where available to reduce impact from new construction. This gives preference to sites within the existing urban fabric.

SS CREDIT 3. BROWNFIELD REDEVELOPMENT (1 POINT)

Build on existing brownfield sites (sites previously developed and then abandoned) wherever possible to rehabilitate sites damaged by prior development and preserve undeveloped sites.

SS CREDITS 4.1, 4.2, 4.3, AND 4.4. ALTERNATIVE TRANSPORTATION (1 POINT EACH)

Credit 4.1 calls for placing buildings to allow access to public transportation. Credit 4.2 is given for providing bicycle storage areas and changing/shower rooms, Credit 4.3 for providing special parking and refueling stations for alternative fuel vehicles, and Credit 4.4 for providing the minimum number of parking spaces required by zoning codes to encourage the use of public/alternative transportation. Like some other LEED credits, Credit 4.4 is at odds with a basic goal of library site design: ensuring that all patrons can find a parking space.

SS CREDITS 5.1 AND 5.2. REDUCED SITE DISTURBANCE (1 POINT EACH)

Credit 5.1 promotes conservation of existing natural areas and restoration of damaged natural areas. Credit 5.2 is given for reducing the area covered by buildings and paving to provide at least 25 percent more open space than is required by local zoning requirements.

SS CREDITS 6.1 AND 6.2. STORMWATER MANAGEMENT (1 POINT EACH)

Credit 6.1 is awarded for controlling stormwater runoff to minimize the impact on natural water flows. This is already required by many zoning codes as a flood control measure. Credit 6.2 is given when pollutants and silt are captured from runoff on-site. Often this is done with *bioswales*—planted areas that filter runoff water and capture chemicals and silt that would otherwise contaminate waterways.

SS CREDITS 7.1 AND 7.2. REDUCE URBAN HEAT ISLAND (1 POINT EACH)

These credits promote using shade trees for paved areas, light-colored paving to reduce daytime heat buildup, and light-colored roofing materials, which not only minimize the urban heat island effect but also lower cooling costs.

SS CREDIT 8. REDUCE LIGHT POLLUTION (1 POINT)

Don't let light from your site trespass onto adjacent properties. Use fixtures that direct light downward, not toward the sky. The second part of this strategy also saves lighting costs by ensuring that the energy used for lighting is utilized efficiently.

Water Efficiency Credits

WE CREDITS 1.1 AND 1.2. WATER EFFICIENT LANDSCAPING (1 POINT EACH)

Credit 1.1 is for reducing usage of potable water for landscape irrigation by 50 percent or for using recycled site water for irrigation. For Credit 1.2, you must eliminate the usage of potable water for landscape irrigation. This can be done by using recycled site water as well as *xeriscaping*—landscaping with drought-tolerant plants.

WE CREDIT 2. INNOVATIVE WASTEWATER STRATEGIES (1 POINT)

Reduce the usage of potable municipal water for the conveyance of sewerage by 50 percent. Use "gray water" captured from roofs, generated by sinks and showers, and the like when high-quality water is not needed. Gray water can be used for toilets and irrigation, though many local plumbing codes don't yet allow this.

WE CREDITS 3.1 AND 3.2. REDUCE WATER USE BY 20 PERCENT AND 30 PERCENT, RESPECTIVELY (1 POINT EACH)

Reduce water use by utilizing water-efficient plumbing fixtures, automatic shutoffs on lavatories, and so forth to reduce the burden on the municipal water system. Efficient plumbing fixtures are becoming more available.

Energy and Atmosphere Credits

EA PREREQUISITE 1. FUNDAMENTAL BUILDING SYSTEMS COMMISSIONING (PREREQUISITE; NO POINTS AWARDED)

This credit mandates that building systems be *commissioned* before the building is occupied. Commissioning is an in-depth verification that all building systems (particularly mechanical and electrical systems) are operating properly. This verification is usually done by an independent third party not part of the design team and is summarized in a commissioning report.

During construction, the mechanical, electrical, and plumbing engineers retained by the architect confirm that the systems installed are generally in conformance with the drawings and specifications. A thorough analysis confirming that the equipment is running exactly as intended is usually beyond the scope of the architect's and engineer's work. This comes as a surprise to many clients. The commissioning process ensures that your building is running as efficiently as possible.

EA PREREQUISITE 2. MINIMUM ENERGY PERFORMANCE (PREREQUISITE; NO POINTS AWARDED)

Design the building to comply with the ASHRAE 90.1 standard or with local energy codes, whichever is more stringent. ASHRAE (American Society of Heating, Refrigeration and Air Conditioning Engineers) has developed an energy efficiency standard that is becoming widely used in this country. Although conforming to this standard can increase construction costs somewhat, it results in lower heating and cooling costs.

EA PREREQUISITE 3. CFC REDUCTION IN HVAC&R EQUIPMENT (PREREQUISITE; NO POINTS AWARDED)

This acronym-laden criterion essentially says that your mechanical equipment—the heating, ventilating, air conditioning, and refrigeration equipment—should not use refrigerants that contain chlorinated fluorocarbons (CFCs; freon is the best-known CFC). This class of compound has been shown to harm the earth's ozone layer and is being phased out of general use.

EA CREDIT 1. OPTIMIZE ENERGY PERFORMANCE (1–10 POINTS)

These points are awarded for increasing energy performance 15–60 percent greater than that required by ASHRAE 90.1 (see EA Prerequisite 2, above). Solar power, ground-source heat recovery, more efficient building insulation, higher-efficiency water heaters, and more efficient lighting can all contribute to this credit.

EA CREDITS 2.1, 2.2, AND 2.3. RENEWABLE ENERGY (1 POINT EACH)

This encourages use of on-site renewable energy sources and offers one point for 5 percent renewable energy usage and additional points for 10 percent and 20 percent renewable energy usage. On-site renewable energy sources might include wind turbines, solar cells, and biomass gas generators. At this time, photovoltaic cells to generate electricity from sunlight are one of the few options available for a library building. The initial cost is relatively high, and they may not make economic sense if their cost cannot be offset by government grants.

EA CREDIT 3. ADDITIONAL BUILDING COMMISSIONING (1 POINT)

This represents a higher level of commissioning than required in the prerequisite portion of this section.

EA CREDIT 4. OZONE PROTECTION (1 POINT)

An additional 1–10 points are available by complying with the Montreal Protocol; this is primarily concerned with utilizing non–ozone harming refrigerants in cooling systems.

EA CREDIT 5. MEASUREMENT AND VERIFICATION (1 POINT)

This credit promotes the development and implementation of a plan to monitor a building's energy usage actively to confirm that energy saving systems are working correctly after the building is in use.

EA CREDIT 6. GREEN POWER (1 POINT)

This credit promotes the use of *green power*—power sold by utility companies that is generated through sustainable means. Green power utilizes the same transmission lines as regular power. This is essentially a higher power rate paid to help subsidize green power generation (e.g., wind power). To qualify for this point, you must enter into a minimum two-year green power contract with a utility company.

Materials and Resources Credits

MR PREREQUISITE 1. STORAGE AND COLLECTION OF RECYCLABLES (PREREQUISITE; NO POINTS AWARDED)

Provide an easily accessible recycling area that serves the entire building and is available to all occupants.

MR CREDITS 1.1, 1.2, AND 1.3. BUILDING REUSE (1 POINT EACH)

Credits are given for reusing all or parts of buildings, varying from 75 percent of existing walls, floor, and roof (1 point); to 100 percent of existing walls, floor, and roof (1 point); to 100 percent of the building shell and 50 percent of the non-structural portion of the building (1 point). The heavy floor loading required for libraries can make reuse of existing structures a challenge. Existing slab-on-grade buildings can often be used if they possess sufficient ceiling height and don't have many interior load-bearing walls.

MR CREDITS 2.1 AND 2.2. CONSTRUCTION WASTE MANAGEMENT (1 POINT EACH)

Credits are awarded for diverting 50 percent or 75 percent of construction debris from landfills. This requires multiple recycling dumpsters on-site and cooperation from the construction contractor.

MR CREDITS 3.1 AND 3.2. RESOURCE REUSE (1 POINT EACH)

These credits promote utilizing reused building materials to reduce the demand for new, virgin materials. One point is given for utilizing 5 percent recycled materials; an additional point is awarded for utilizing 10 percent recycled materials. It can be difficult to find salvaged or reused materials in large enough and consistent enough amounts for anything but the smallest library building projects. A notable exception is structural steel; much of the steel used in North America is made of recycled material.

MR CREDITS 4.1 AND 4.2. RECYCLED CONTENT (1 POINT EACH)

These credits promote utilizing reused building materials with various percentages of recycled materials. Many carpets and upholstery fabrics now on the market feature high percentages of recycled materials and are good ways to increase the percentage of recycled contents in the library.

MR CREDITS 5.1 AND 5.2. REGIONAL MATERIALS (1 POINT EACH)

Points are awarded for utilizing increasing percentages of materials that are extracted and manufactured within 500 miles of the project site. This saves energy otherwise expended in the transport of building materials.

MR CREDIT 6. RAPIDLY RENEWABLE MATERIALS (1 POINT)

This point is achieved when a minimum of 5 percent of the project is composed of materials classified as rapidly renewable. In this context, "rapidly renewable" means made from plants that are grown and harvested within a ten-year cycle. Some of the more common building materials that fall in this category are bamboo and linoleum flooring. Bamboo flooring can easily be used in library areas where carpet's acoustic properties are not of high importance.

MR CREDIT 7. CERTIFIED WOOD (1 POINT)

To qualify for this point, 50 percent of the wood used in the project must come from forests managed in accordance with the Forest Stewardship Council's criteria, which are intended to ensure that wood is produced in a sustainable manner.

Indoor Environmental Quality Credits

EQ PREREQUISITE 1. MINIMUM INDOOR AIR QUALITY PERFORMANCE (PREREQUISITE; NO POINTS AWARDED)

Meeting a standard of high indoor air quality contributes to the health and well-being of the occupants. Providing adequate levels of fresh air as well as appropriate filtration and humidity reduces the levels of indoor chemical contaminants, carbon dioxide, and microbial contamination. You've probably heard of "sick building syndrome"; meeting appropriate indoor air quality standards prevents most sick building problems.

EQ PREREQUISITE 2. ENVIRONMENTAL TOBACCO SMOKE CONTROL (PREREQUISITE; NO POINTS AWARDED)

Altogether eliminates nonsmokers' exposure to tobacco smoke.

EQ CREDIT 1. CARBON DIOXIDE MONITORING (1 POINT)

A buildup of carbon dioxide inside a building can make people tired and less productive and has been associated with increased levels of illness. Monitoring carbon dioxide levels alerts building engineers that indoor air quality is not up to appropriate standards and that the ventilation system needs to be modified or adjusted.

EQ CREDIT 2. VENTILATION EFFECTIVENESS (1 POINT)

Specifying the minimum amount of fresh air that must be brought into a building ensures an adequate supply of fresh air for all building occupants.

EQ CREDITS 3.1 AND 3.2. CONSTRUCTION PHASE INDOOR AIR QUALITY MANAGEMENT PLAN (1 POINT EACH)

Credit 3.1 is intended to keep indoor air quality levels at acceptable standards during the construction period to protect the health of construction workers. Credit 3.2 requires that the air in the new building be thoroughly flushed prior to building occupancy. Flushing indoor air basically means that fresh air is circulated through the building at a high rate before the building is occupied. This helps reduce the building occupants' exposure to construction phase pollution.

EQ CREDITS 4.1, 4.2, 4.3, AND 4.4. LOW-EMITTING MATERIALS (ADHESIVES, PAINTS, CARPETING, AND COMPOSITE WOOD, RESPECTIVELY) (1 POINT EACH)

These criteria encourage the use of low-emitting materials—materials that do not give off appreciable amounts of air contaminants—throughout the building. Carpeting, adhesives, paints, plywood, and a host of other building materials were found to emit significant amounts of dangerous chemicals, especially in the first few months after construction. Low-emitting versions of these materials are increasingly easy to find and should be specified as a matter of course in construction projects.

EQ CREDIT 5. INDOOR CHEMICAL AND POLLUTANT SOURCE CONTROL (1 POINT)

Earning this credit requires protecting building occupants from tracked-in dirt as well as hazardous chemicals used for cleaning or other purposes. Walk-off mats can trap dirt tracked in on people's shoes, preventing it from eventually becoming airborne dust. Added ventilation can be provided in places where chemicals are used, such as janitor's closets and kitchens. Combined with a sufficient supply of fresh air, these measures can make buildings much healthier places to be.

EQ CREDITS 6.1 AND 6.2. CONTROLLABILITY OF SYSTEMS (IN PERIMETER SPACES AND NONPERIMETER SPACES, RESPECTIVELY) (1 POINT EACH)

For perimeter spaces, these credits encourage design that allows individual control of local environments by providing sufficient operable windows and lighting controls. For nonperimeter spaces, the design should allow occupants to control local lighting, ventilation, and temperature.

For just about every library we design, we hear the same request: Give us operable windows. It's not as easy as it sounds. Typical mechanical systems are not set up to allow windows to be opened or closed randomly. We all know the archetypal parental reprimand: Close the door, I'm not paying to heat the whole outdoors! This applies in the case of most traditional mechanical systems; if a window is to be opened and the building is to remain efficient, the local mechanical system must be shut off. This can be accomplished in smaller spaces like offices by incorporating sensors that detect when a window has been opened and shut off heating/air conditioning in that space. In larger public spaces it can be more challenging. Providing enough mechanical zones and controls within a building to facilitate operable windows can be an expensive proposition. It's a good goal, however, since people are happiest when they have some control over their environment.

EQ CREDITS 7.1 AND 7.2. THERMAL COMFORT (1 POINT EACH)

Credit 7.1 requires that inhabited spaces remain within thermal comfort standards as defined by ASHRAE. Credit 7.2 requires that there be a permanent temperature and humidity monitoring system configured to provide building operators control over thermal comfort and humidification systems.

EQ CREDITS 8.1 AND 8.2. DAYLIGHT AND VIEWS (1 POINT EACH)

Credit 8.1 requires that 75 percent of spaces within a building have access to daylight and views of the outdoors. Credit 8.2 raises the required percentage of spaces with daylight and views to 90 percent. Daylight is important to people's well-being; views of the outdoors connect them to the outside environment and are equally beneficial. A well-designed daylighting plan can save a significant amount of energy that would otherwise be devoted to artificial lighting. Other options like light-colored surfaces and appropriate ceiling designs can also help distribute natural light within a space.

There are several library-specific questions to address when utilizing daylighting. Glare on computer monitors can be problematic, and ultraviolet light must be excluded to protect the collection. Allowing too much direct sunlight into a building promotes heat gain and can increase cooling bills. We are left with a balancing act: provide as much daylight and outside view as possible without causing an unacceptable number of compromises to library operations. The easiest way to light a library would be to have no windows at all and provide completely uniform lighting with indirect light fixtures (think "big box store" here). It would be easy and it would be uniform, but it's not what people want. Experience has shown that people generally prefer more natural light and are willing (and happy) to put up with less than perfect lighting conditions as long as natural light is available. At night, the rules change; there is no reason to design compromises into a fully artificial lighting layout.

Innovation and Design Process Credits

ID CREDIT 1. INNOVATION IN DESIGN (1–4 POINTS)

There are no specific criteria for these credits; they are intended to let designers pursue new avenues of sustainable design. Whether new design features are credited is up to the USGBC reviewer. The design team identifies the intent of the innovation, the proposed requirements for compliance, and the design approach that meets those requirements.

ID CREDIT 2. LEED ACCREDITED PROFESSIONAL (1–4 POINTS)

To achieve this credit, at least one principal in the design team must be LEED accredited.

By just skimming this outline of the LEED system, you can see what I mean by describing LEED as a holistic structure. Sustainable design is more than saving energy and recycling materials; it implies a different way of looking at the environment and the impact our actions have on it. Sustainability is a choice, and ultimately it may be our only choice.

This All Sounds Great, but What Does It Cost?

When I first began learning about sustainable design, I attended seminars on sustainable strategies. One of the presenters was employed by a university and gave a compelling presentation on the benefits and need for sustainable design. Responding to a question from the audience at the end of his talk, he told us that sustainable design was "no more expensive than traditional design." Maybe too many years in business have made me cynical, but I distinctly remember thinking that this guy had been in school too long.

His comment may be true for a residence or other small project where sustainability is a labor of love for the client, but for most projects there is a premium to be paid. The upcharge depends on the strategies employed. For many projects, a LEED rating can probably be achieved at a premium of 5–7 percent over what you would have paid for traditional construction. That premium will most likely be recovered many times over during the useful life of the building through lower utility costs.

Yes, many if not most LEED projects have a higher first cost. That is of critical concern for those designing and selling strip centers and condominiums. Without government pressure, few of those private sector players have an incentive to produce sustainable projects. Libraries are somewhat different; these are multigenerational buildings that serve large segments of our society. Libraries are increasingly becoming civic centers; we are setting an example. We must set the right example by "doing the right thing."

A Final Note

Find out if your architect is LEED accredited. If not, ask why. Even if you aren't planning for a LEED certified building, sustainable design principles should be incorporated into every project.

Chapter 14

Project Costs and Building Costs

Raising the financial resources to build a library is never easy. No matter how big or small your project, you are going to need to know just how much library your money can buy.

This chapter is adapted from "Understanding Project Costs and Building Costs," by Rick McCarthy, which originally appeared as *Bottom Line: Managing Library Finances* 17, no. 1 (2004); Emerald Group Publishing Ltd.

What Do Libraries Cost?

Sometimes the budgeting process must begin well before a design has been established or even before an architect has been hired. How can you come up with an early estimate of what a project will cost? There is usually plenty of anecdotal information regarding library construction costs. Unfortunately, anecdotal information is often out of date, inaccurate, misleading, or not applicable to your situation.

The State Library of Iowa has an effective website with much information useful for library professionals. One section—"Library building projects—past and present"—contains an Excel compilation of data on public libraries built in Iowa from 1981 through 2003. We looked at the data for new libraries built between 1999 and 2002 and noted that those costs varied from $18 to $217 per square foot. Although $217 would not be an unbelievably high figure, $18 per square foot is impossibly low. The wild swing in the cost figures does not reflect laxity on the part of the Iowa State Library; it no doubt reflects the data their member libraries submitted. The lesson is that people have different ideas about what the "cost" of a building is, and that what data there is may not be compiled (or submitted) in a uniform manner.

Suppose you are just beginning to investigate what you are likely to spend for a new library building. A library building consultant has given you a ballpark idea of how big your library must be to meet your service goals. You might start by calling several nearby libraries to find out just how much their recently built buildings cost per square foot. It is nearly certain that you will get answers that vary; different people use different yardsticks to measure the cost of their projects. One number may include new furniture for the library while another does not. One number may include site acquisition costs while another omits them. These vagaries make it difficult to estimate how much your project is likely to cost if you simply work from your neighbors' costs.

There are reference sources to help you arrive at a first guess regarding the price. The RSMeans *Building Construction Cost Data,* commonly used in the United States, is useful but requires care since it represents average construction costs; there is no "one size fits all" in the world of library construction. The Means data book also has information to help you adjust your "average" library cost to match costs in your geographic area.

The adjustment for geographic area provides an interesting comparison of library costs in different parts of the country. Before you read on, please remember that these cost numbers are out of date. Look for the trends in this data, not at the numbers themselves. According to Means 2003 data, an "average" library costs approximately $106 per square foot before geographic area multipliers are applied. The geographic multipliers account for the differing costs of construction in different parts of the country. Applying those factors yields the following costs for the same library in different locations:

Far Rockaway, New York	geographic multiplier of 1.306 yields a building cost of $138.43/square foot
Kingman, Arizona	geographic multiplier of 0.84 yields a building cost of $89.04/square foot
Akron, Ohio	geographic multiplier of 0.994 yields a building cost of $105.36/square foot

These numbers do not include costs for site acquisition, site development, furniture, professional fees, and several other significant items. The wide variance between construction costs for the sample geographic areas illustrates one of the pitfalls of utilizing anecdotal information. Inflation is another factor that can render anecdotal information useless. With any appreciable amount of inflation, building cost data quickly becomes dated.

Our architectural practice is based in northern Illinois. In our area as of this writing, a new library building and its associated site work (not including site acquisition, equipment, or furniture) is likely to cost $190–$220 per square foot (in 2006 dollars). I use $200 for the following example.

An Example

How much library will we get for our money? It seems like an easy question. Let's imagine that you have $4 million available for a library construction project, and you have determined that $200 per square foot is an appropriate cost for your area. $4 million divided by $200 per square foot equals a library of approximately 20,000 square feet, right? *Not necessarily.* . . . First, you must answer a critical question: What percentage of your project funding actually goes toward bricks and mortar?

In our experience, most clients (and many architects) underestimate how much of their budget will be devoted to project-related expenses beyond the costs of the "bricks and mortar." As often as not, clients think of their dollars as going toward the *building budget,* but their dollars actually make up the *project budget.* The building budget covers the bricks and mortar along with the labor to put them in place. The project budget consists of the cost of the building itself plus the costs of all those other things that make up a complete construction project. The difference between these numbers makes all the difference in how much library you will get for your dollar.

Let's go through a set of hypothetical numbers to see the relationship between a building budget and a project budget. For the spreadsheet in figure 14-1, we have adjusted the building budget (the bricks and mortar part) to arrive at a total project budget of $4 million. (All the following numbers, including professional fees, are examples only and may not apply to your project.)

The spreadsheet is fairly typical of an initial project estimate. Later in the design process the architect may provide refined estimates many pages long with detailed takeoffs covering every major building component. At this early stage of the process, however, that kind of detail is not possible, since there is not yet a building design to work with.

Here's something to think about: Some of the most important decisions regarding the project—such as the amount of a referendum—may be made before you really know much about the building you propose to build. An accurate initial assessment of *all* the costs associated with your project is required to ensure that you meet your goals.

The spreadsheet includes some line item costs that may not apply to you. Maybe you already have money set aside to cover some of them. Some of the legal costs may be covered by funds already in hand. Perhaps your current operating budget is sufficiently large to purchase the additional items you want for your opening-day collection. Whatever your particular situation, the spreadsheet will alert you to some of the kinds of cost you should anticipate.

Your Bottom Line

In this example, $2,624,739 (approximately 66 percent) of your $4 million actually goes toward the construction cost of your new building. Without additional funding, the 20,000-square-foot building you were expecting will actually have an area more in the range of 13,100 square feet. It is pretty simple, if your initial budget was set at $4 million, to match the amount of money you have available to spend; you're going to get a nice new library of approximately 13,100 square feet. Note that this number includes new furniture and at least some of the computers and equipment you need for a modern library. On the other hand, you'll have to start looking for more money if you began with a needs analysis that stipulates a library of 20,000 square feet to meet your service goals. We looked at some of our current actual library projects and found that the percentage of the budget going directly toward bricks and mortar varied from around 65 percent to 80 percent. When you first begin testing the financial waters, 65–70 percent might be a good place to start.

Remember to take these numbers with a grain of salt. If you have $4 million to spend, you may get a library significantly larger or smaller than 13,700 square feet. This scenario reflects a specific collection of items included in this project cost. You may not require many of the items listed here. Your mileage *will* vary.

Apples and Oranges

Exercise care when comparing costs of different library projects. In this example, the *construction cost* of the library is expressed by $2,624,739 / 13,124 square feet,

Conceptual Project Cost Estimate

Conceptual Project Cost Estimates And Fee Analysis For A Hypothetical Project With An Overall Budget Of $4,000,000		
	Cost of New Construction and Site Development	$2,624,739
Professional Fees	**Professional Fees** Architectural, Mechanical Engineering, Electrical Engineering, Plumbing Engineering and Civil Engineering based upon estimated construction cost	$223,103
	Interior Design Fees (Library Furniture, Commercial Furniture and Stacks) Design, preparation of bidding documents and bidding	$25,985
	On-Site observation allowance for Architect's on-site time	$60,000
	Materials Testing	$7,800
Misc. Costs	**Soil Borings**	$5,000
	Estimated Permit Costs Village review fees, utility tie-in's	$20,000
	Environmental Surveying	$5,000
	Moving	$20,000
	Site Surveying	$5,000
	Opening Day Collection	$100,000
	Professional Cost Estimating	$7,000
	Phone And Data	$60,000
	Book Security System	$100,000
	Legal Fees	$10,000
	Equipment - copiers, fax machines, misc. library equipment etc.	$100,000
Subtotal, Miscellaneous Costs and Fees		$748,888
Estimated Cost per Square Foot Of New Construction (Including Site Development):		$200
Estimated Area of New Construction	Estimated using above per square foot cost against the New Construction Allowance	13,124 SF
Furniture Allowance $/SF of building area		$22
Estimated Furniture Cost		$288,721
Project Contingency and inflation of 10.00%		$363,636
Estimated Project Cost	Construction Cost + Fees + Miscellaneous Expenses	$4,000,000

Asbestos and buried tank remediation (if required) not included
Site development costs are included

Figure 14-1

Sample conceptual project cost estimate and fee analysis

yielding $200 per square foot. The *project cost* of the same building is $4,000,000/13,124 square feet, resulting in $305 per square foot. When asking someone about the cost of their new library, you never know what number you are getting: project cost, building cost, or some mixture of the two. As often as not, even the clients don't really know what the numbers mean; someone on the design or construction team told them that their building cost "X" dollars per square foot without really explaining the basis used for determining the cost. When evaluating cost estimates for different projects, be sure you are comparing apples with apples.

The Importance of Contingency

Note that figure 14-1 has a line showing a 10 percent contingency, which in this example amounts to more than $360,000. Contingencies are required to cover all the unknowns that crop up during the course of a project as well as inflation between the time you go for project funding and the time bids are taken. The earlier you are in the building process, the higher the contingency should be. At the conceptual stage of a project, we usually add 10 percent. This gets somewhat reduced as the design progresses and the cost estimates are refined.

Summary

When you begin planning for a construction project, it is important that you understand the difference between construction cost and project costs. The additional costs that make up the difference between building costs and project costs must be included to ensure that your funding matches your goals.

Every project is different. If you are planning an addition to a historic Carnegie library, you should be prepared for significant costs for asbestos remediation and upgrades to the old mechanical and electrical systems. A new building on a greenfield site with good soil conditions and easy access to power, sewer, and water will probably yield a lower project cost per square foot.

Building Cost versus Building Size

Larger buildings tend to be more efficient to construct. Many project costs such as professional fees, surveys, and testing are proportionally smaller for larger buildings. Table 14-1 gives some comparative cost analyses for hypothetical projects ranging from $1 million to $10 million. Note that the project cost per square foot varies rather dramatically depending on the project size, another reason for exercising caution when comparing cost numbers from different projects.

Don't Forget the Operating Costs

There is no reason to hesitate quizzing your architect about what has been done to minimize the costs of running your new or remodeled

Table 14-1

Sample cost analyses

Overall project cost	Project dollars going toward construction	Resulting building area	Construction cost per sq ft	Project cost per sq ft
$1 million	$462,094	2,310 sq ft	$200	$433
$2 million	$1,205,501	6,028 sq ft	$200	$331
$4 million	$2,624,739	13,124 sq ft	$200	$304
$10 million	$7,198,064	35,990 sq ft	$200	$277

library once it is built. Sometimes what seem like small changes in the design of a building can produce dramatically different operational costs. It is difficult to predict utility costs for new buildings. Many variables are difficult to predict: the changing costs of gas and electricity, the number of hours per week the facility is open, how the climate will be in a particular year, how much your systems will cost to run. As unscientific as it sounds, the best measure is often to find nearby libraries of about the same size and ask them about their utility bills.

Epilogue

*We shall not cease from exploration
And the end of all our exploring
Will be to arrive where we started
And know the place for the first time.*

—T. S. Eliot

The Great Circle Route

We have come full circle. We began by talking about architects and what they do. Next, we looked at the parts of a typical architectural project and how they might apply to your situation. In the end, we returned to architects and looked at how you might find and hire one. Throughout all of this, there has been one prime purpose: to help you build a better library.

An architect is one of the many resources you use to accomplish your goal. Selecting the right resource for the job, and knowing how to use it, is a good first step for any project.

I hope this book will be of use to you. Our society is changing rapidly, and the role of the library within it is changing as well. It remains to be seen how libraries will evolve. In fact, the only thing we know for sure is that the library will evolve, must evolve to keep pace with the growing technology of the electronic transfer of information. Within the space of a decade or two, the workings of libraries have advanced from nineteenth-century technology to that of the twenty-first century. This evolution requires that new libraries be built and existing ones be adapted to enable them to take on these new roles. It is the partnerships among library boards, library professionals, and architects that will help make possible the birth of this new kind of library.

I welcome your questions and comments. Please feel free to send them to me via the publisher or via e-mail at r.mccarthy@library-architect.com. I wish you good luck in your building endeavors.

Semper Aedifica!

Sample Request for Qualifications: Architectural Services

This form can be sent to architectural firms that have expressed an interest in your project.

Request for Qualifications for Architectural Services
Roosevelt Library District

The Roosevelt Library District is seeking specific qualifications from interested Architectural firms that are capable of providing professional services for the siting, design, and construction of a new library. The library district serves a population of 90,000 and is currently housed in a 45,000-square-foot building located at 429 Augusta Avenue, Ourtown. Based on the recommendations of the Library Building Consultant, it is anticipated that the new library will be approximately 70,000 square feet in area.

I. Description of the Architect Procurement Process

The process for procurement of Architect services will proceed in two stages.

A. Submission of Written Qualifications

The Library Board will review and evaluate the written responses to the Request for Qualifications (RFQ) in accordance with the evaluation criteria identified in Attachment A. The Library Board will select no more than three qualified Architects to proceed to the oral interview stage of the procurement process. [*Limit the number of firms to be interviewed to three or four at the most.*]

B. Oral Interview

Each of the selected qualified Architects will participate in a detailed oral interview to discuss more fully how their approach to this project satisfies the evaluation criteria set forth in Attachment A. In addition, Architects will be required to answer questions posed by the Selection Committee. It will be the sole responsibility of the Selection Committee to rank the candidates in order of qualification on the basis of the evaluation of the written responses to the RFQ and oral responses received during the interview process. The top-ranking candidate shall then be invited to proceed to the negotiation stage. [*If your state mandates a qualifications-based selection (QBS) approach, you might want to state that the final selection will be based on QBS procedures. See chapter 11 for an overview of QBS.*]

II. Site Visits / Facility Tours

The Library Director will be available to answer questions about the proposed site and operation of the present library. All Architects are encouraged to evaluate the library data contained in the RFQ carefully and visit the potential site(s) as well as the existing facility to enhance their understanding of the project. Please contact the Library Director to schedule site visits.

III. Scope of Services Desired

The professional services of the Architect will be based on Document B141, the standard AIA Owner/Architect agreement, and shall include the following: [*Be sure to state any special requirements that are not covered as part of the "basic services" of the standard Owner/Architect contract. You can obtain copies of the standard contract from the AIA.*]

A. Phase I: pre-referendum services [*If your project is not funded by a referendum, delete references to phases I and II.*]

1. Site selection/architectural programming/predesign

    a. Programming shall incorporate and refine the program produced by the Library Building Consultant.

    b. The Library District shall provide the Architect detailed information about the existing site utilities. This will include a boundary survey, topographic information, and a phase I environmental analysis. [*Environmental analyses may be required for your project. If you are in doubt, contact your local building authorities. They can tell you where to get additional information.*]

2. Schematic design and cost estimate

    a. At the close of the schematic design phase, the Architect shall submit a project cost estimate prepared by an independent, professional cost estimator. [*The cost estimate by an independent professional estimator is optional and is by no means standard practice in the industry. In smaller communities, there may be no professional estimators available.*]

    b. The Architect shall provide a scale model of the proposed library on the site. This model shall be of such quality as to enable it to be displayed to the public during the referendum drive. [*Models are optional and can be costly.*]

    c. The Architect shall provide at least two renderings of the proposed library on the site. The renderings shall be mounted on illustration board and be of such quality as to enable them to be displayed to the public during the referendum.

3. Referendum services

    Members of the design team who are familiar with the design shall be available to attend at least three public meetings, where they will answer public questions regarding the project.

B. Phase II (Post-referendum services, contingent on passage of a building referendum)

1. Design development

    At the close of the design development phase, the Architect shall submit a project cost estimate prepared by an independent, professional cost estimator.

2. Construction documents

3. Bidding and negotiation

4. Construction phase

5. Postconstruction services

IV. Project Size and Individual Characteristics

Detailed information regarding programming requirements for library services is contained in the report submitted by the Library Building Consultant. Copies of this report are available for $20 each (nonrefundable). Contact the Library Director to obtain copies of the report. The facility shall meet all requirements of the Americans with Disabilities Act.

ATTACHMENT A

Evaluation Criteria

The following criteria will be used to evaluate the written submissions of each Architect's qualifications. The comments of the Architect's previous clients will also be considered. (These are not ranked in order of importance.)

A. Project Management

1. There shall be a clear assignment of responsibilities for various project tasks to specific individuals. All individuals with major responsibilities for the project's design, bidding specification, and follow-through should be identified at the oral interview.

2. The Architect shall have a demonstrated ability to observe construction and handle field changes and other contingencies that may arise during construction.

3. The Architect shall be able to demonstrate experience providing effective management, design, and monitoring services on past projects.

4. The Architect shall demonstrate an ability to complete projects within budget and according to schedule.

5. The Architect's responsiveness to the specific user goals identified in the RFQ.

6. The quality of communication skills and the effectiveness of the project manager and on-site construction representative from your firm.

7. The ability to coordinate project construction with contractors, equipment suppliers, and library personnel.

B. Technical Approach; The following items will be considered:

1. The Architect shall exhibit an understanding of library design, existing conditions, systems, operations, and schedules.

2. Qualifications of the design professionals.

3. The number of past library projects completed by the Architect that are similar to this one in scope or complexity.

4. The quality and performance of Architect's past projects. This shall be evaluated by the Board during walk-throughs of several of the Architect's completed buildings and interviews with former clients.

ATTACHMENT B

Project Time Line

Activity	Date
Issue Architectural RFQs	_____
Written Proposals due no later than 1:00 p.m.	_____
Written Proposals evaluated by Library Board	_____
Three Architectural firms selected for short list and notified of oral interview	_____
Facility Tours	_____
Oral Interviews (approximately 1 hour each) by Project Evaluation Team	_____
Selection Committee's recommendation to the Library Board	_____
Contract negotiations with selected Architect	_____
Selection of Architectural firm	_____
Notification of Architectural firm and beginning of schematic design	_____
Programming and schematic design complete	_____
Referendum activities begin	_____
Referendum	_____
Building design resumed (contingent on passage of referendum)	_____
Beginning of construction	_____
Estimated date of substantial completion	_____

[Make your best guess regarding the project time line. You may only know a few of the dates with any certainty. Even if you only know the dates of the selection of the architect and of the referendum, the information will help the architect evaluate office staffing requirements. Be sure to specify if you must take occupancy of the building by a certain date.]

ATTACHMENT C

Submittal Requirements

Applicants must submit responses to the following:

Written material should be sent to the building committee of the Roosevelt Library, 1928 Hoover Place, Ourtown. Submittals must be received before 1:00 p.m., April 1, 2008.

[*Keep your requests for information short and specific. Avoid philosophical essay questions. They tend to make respondents more concerned with trying to tell you what they think you want to hear instead of sticking to the facts. Lists of required submittals should be concise to ensure that you receive similar proposals from each firm.*]

I. **Outline for Qualifications**

Please provide the following information:

A. Firm name/address

B. General history of the firm, including but not limited to

1. Number of years in business

2. Type of ownership, and name(s) of owners

3. Type of organization

4. Geographical area of operations

5. Professional affiliations

6. Amounts and kinds of professional insurance carried

C. Personnel in your present organization

1. Who are the principals in your organization?

2. What are the size and composition of your organization?

3. Please include resumes of personnel you propose to assign to this project.

D. What types of special consultant services not provided by your firm will the Library need to obtain?

E. What additional consultants would you propose to hire to supplement your firm's basic Architectural services? Please provide their names and relevant experience.

F. List any additional related services your firm can provide, such as interior design, energy management, etc.

G. Discuss your firm's experience with sustainable design.

II. **Past Performance**

A. Please indicate up to five similar-size library buildings you have designed in the past ten years. Including location, size, and cost.

B. Indicate buildings your firm currently has in progress. Include location, size, and cost of each.

C. List the total cost of change orders on each of the above projects. [*This is often asked on RFQs. Because they can arise for any number of reasons, change orders and their costs do not necessarily have a direct correlation with the quality of the architect's service. If you ask this question, give the architect an opportunity to discuss the reasons for the change orders.*]

D. Considering previous commitments you have made for Architectural services, can the work on the project be scheduled in your office for immediate participation on selection as the project Architect?

III. Supplemental Information

A. Please provide other pertinent information that you feel makes you qualified for the proposed project. Limit supplemental information to five typewritten pages. [*Place strict limits on the amount of supplemental information you will accept. Without limitations, some architects are brief and concise while others overwhelm you with every scrap of information they feel could possibly be to their advantage. These kinds of disparities can make it difficult to compare proposals.*]

B. Provide references that may be contacted for each of the projects listed. Include name, title, phone number, and address for each contact person.

C. It is the intent of the Library Board to tour several buildings designed by each of the potential Architectural firms. [*Visits to completed projects can be an important part of the selection process. Try to visit at least one project that is five years old or more to evaluate how buildings designed by the architect are holding up. Remember, however, that if you don't like one of the designs you see, it could still be a successful project that gave the client exactly what was wanted—design is very subjective.*]

Sample Request for Proposals:
Construction Manager as Advisor Services

This form may need to be modified to conform to local regulations.

Request for Proposals for Construction Manager as Advisor Services
Roosevelt Library District

June 9, 2008

Dear Sir / Madam:

The Roosevelt Library District invites you to submit a reply for Request for Proposal for Construction Management Services. Please address all responses to

Harold Hopkins
Director
Roosevelt Library District
Yourtown, Yourstate
Yourzip

Proposals will be received until 10:00 a.m., local time, July 1, 2008.

It is the intention of the Roosevelt Library District to consider these proposals during July 2008. A short list of Construction Managers will be selected using the criteria listed in this RFP, and interviews will be conducted in August 2008. The Roosevelt Library District may make such investigations as they deem necessary to determine the ability of the Construction Manager to perform the work, and the vendor shall furnish to the Selection Committee all such information for this purpose as they may request. The Roosevelt Library District reserves the right to reject any or all proposals if the evidence submitted by, or investigation of, such Construction Manager fails to satisfy the Roosevelt Library District that such Construction Manager is properly qualified to carry out the obligations of the contract and to complete work contemplated therein. The Roosevelt Library District reserves the right to waive any irregularities or minor defects in the proposal and to accept the proposal that is in the best interest of the Roosevelt Library District. Conditional proposals will not be accepted.

Please address any questions to
Your Architect
Phone: XXX-XXXX
FAX: XXX-XXXX
E-mail: yourarchitect@yourarch.com

PURPOSE

Roosevelt Library District is issuing this Request for Proposal (RFP) for professional services. The purpose of this RFP is to solicit quotations for providing professional

Construction Management services for all construction services for the project described below. The Roosevelt Library District hopes to enter into a contract with a responsible firm for such services and accordingly is seeking certain information whereby such service capabilities shall be evaluated.

SELECTION TIME FRAME / SELECTION CRITERIA

Proposals will be received until 10:00 a.m., local time, July 1, 2008. After that time, the City, Library Trustees, Library Director, and Architects will review all submissions. It is anticipated that interviews with selected firms will be held in August 2008.

The following factors will be used in arriving at the selection of a Construction Management firm, including but not limited to:

A. Qualifications

B. General experience

C. Specific record of accomplishments with similar projects

D. Skills and abilities of personnel

E. Use of outside consultants

F. Performance data, including but not limited to cost control, and scheduling procedures

G. Workload and scheduling availability to start work on the project

H. Fees

I. Experience working with area contractors

J. References

The contract may be awarded to the most responsible firm whose proposal will be, on an overall basis, the most advantageous to the Roosevelt Library District. Qualifications, experience, performance, and cost factors will be considered as elements of a responsible proposal at the sole discretion of the Roosevelt Library District. Cost alone shall not be the determining factor. The District's decision shall be final and not subject to recourse by any firm, person, or corporation. The Roosevelt Library District reserves the right to reject any and all proposals and/or waive nonsubstantive deficiencies.

SCOPE OF WORK

This RFP is for Construction Manager as Advisor services for all construction trades in conjunction with the referenced project. This project is anticipated to be an addition to the existing Roosevelt Library District library building. The existing library has an area of approximately 9,000 square feet. The proposed addition is anticipated to have an area of approximately 20,000–25,000 square feet.

It is estimated that the drawings will be released for bidding in April 2008. This will not be a "fast-track" project.

The existing library will remain in operation during the construction of the addition. After the addition is completed, library operations will be relocated into the addition and the existing library building will be remodeled. When remodeling of the original library is complete, that part of the building will be reopened to the public.

The estimated amount for contractor trade work is approximately $X,000,000, including contingencies.

The funding for this project is contingent on the passage of a building referendum tentatively scheduled for November 2007. Prior to the referendum, the Construction Manager will assist with cost estimating and value engineering. It is anticipated that, in the event of a successful referendum, construction will begin in spring 2008 and will be complete in spring 2009.

It is the District's intention to utilize the Construction Management firm's ability and expertise in lieu of a general contractor. The Construction Management firm will coordinate and handle all work necessary to ensure that contracts between the Library District and all applicable subcontractors are met.

It is the District's intention to enter into a contract with a Construction Management firm as soon as possible.

The Construction Manager will assist the District and the Architect/Engineer through preconstruction and then manage construction. Responsibilities of the Construction Manager include, but are not limited to, the following:

Post-referendum Phase, Preconstruction Phase

- Develop a preliminary estimate from the Architect's existing schematic design documents. Work with the Architect to refine the budget and estimate, incorporating value engineering ideas that have been developed in conjunction with the Architect to bring the project into budget incorporating available project funds.
- Develop a project schedule(s) to reflect team member contributions, construction activities, and critical occupancy dates.
- Conduct ongoing value engineering to identify opportunities for enhancing the value of the project. This effort will analyze the item or system in question relative to first cost (to furnish and install) in deference to maintenance, utility costs, durability, and cost to replace.
- Develop estimates from design development documents and bidding documents. Refine the budgets and estimates throughout preconstruction to reflect value engineering ideas that have been developed in conjunction with the Architect.
- Refine project schedule to reflect team member contributions, construction activities, and critical occupancy dates.
- Identify "long-lead" items and coordinate bids so that the schedule is not compromised.
- Work with Architect/Engineer to develop cost estimates as required for determining the amount of the referendum.

Bidding/Contract Award Phase

- Assist in preparation of General and Special Conditions.
- Prepare a progress schedule and scope of work for inclusion in bid documents.
- Prepare a cash flow schedule.
- Submit a list of recommended bidders for all categories of work to the Roosevelt Library District and Architect for prior review and approval.

- Provide instructions and scope of work details to all invited bidders.
- Solicit, receive, and analyze all bids. Develop a bid tabulation form and list award recommendations.
- Assist the Roosevelt Library District in preparing contracts and purchase orders with same to be "held" by the District.

Construction

- Provide home office and job site administration.
- Manage all trades.
- Manage shop drawing and submittal review process and ensure expediting of same.
- Review requests for information, requests for proposals, and subcontractor's responses to same.
- Hold and chair weekly progress meetings.
- Attend regular Building Committee meetings to be held approximately once a month.
- Review and recommend pay requests for payment by the District in conjunction with the Facility Committee.
- Obtain bonds and lien waivers from subcontractors.
- Provide monthly progress reports addressing any cost or schedule changes.
- Update cash flow requirements.
- Expedite substantial completion and occupancy certificates.
- Obtain closeout documents such as as-builts, guarantees/warranties, and operation and maintenance manuals.
- Assist in obtaining inspections by governing authorities with jurisdiction and act as the District's representative with local municipalities and the applicable fire prevention authorities.
- Assist the Library with moves.
- Prepare a punch list and expedite completion.

Postconstruction Phase

- Coordinate and expedite the resolution of construction-related problems.
- Coordinate and expedite the repair/replacement of items covered under guarantees/warranties.
- Conduct follow-up review of the complete facility to help ensure satisfactory performance of materials and systems.

Comment: The District will not consider Construction Management firms who propose to act as a subcontractor on this project or who propose to assign Construction Management tasks to other firms.

SUBMITTAL REQUIREMENTS

Proposals shall address the following:

I. **Business Organization**

    A. Firm name, business address, and telephone.

    B. Name and title of contact person.

    C. Number of years your organization has been in business under its present business name.

    D. Type of ownership: Partnership, Corporation, or Other.

    E. If a corporation, please provide the following:

        1. Date of incorporation

        2. State of incorporation

        3. Principal officers

    F. If other than a corporation, describe the organization and name its principals.

    G. Have you ever failed to complete work awarded to you? If so, explain when, where, and why this happened.

    H. Provide a statement of the company's financial condition and financial references.

II. **Similar Project Construction Management Experience**

    A. Please indicate what percentage of projects you do on the following basis:

        1. Construction management

        2. Lump sum general contract—design/bid/build

        3. Design/build

    B. Please list the dollar value of work completed in this area in the past five years under the Construction Manager as Agent approach.

    C. Please list the number of public sector/municipal projects you have completed with an individual construction cost of $5 million or more.

    D. Using the criteria of public sector/municipal valued over $1 million, list a minimum of five similar projects completed within the past five years for which you have served as Construction Manager. (Do not list projects where you have served as a lump sum general contractor or consultant.) For each project listed, include project name and address, year completed, construction cost, type of project (New, Renovation, Addition, Replacement), and a project reference (Name, Position, Telephone Number).

III. **Construction Management Capabilities and Services**

    A. Describe your approach to a Construction Manger/Owner/Architect/Engineer team and your relationship to each team member.

    B. Please indicate projects you have been hired for prior to the start of working construction documents.

C. Briefly describe how your firm performs the following services:
1. Cost estimating
2. Cost control
3. Quality control
4. Drawing and specification review
5. Value engineering
6. Scheduling in preconstruction and construction phases
7. Approach to bid packaging and the purchase of trade contracts
8. Coordination of various trade contractors
9. Safety programs, labor relations, other items of interest
10. Sustainable construction practices

D. Describe your in-house capabilities to implement the above services related to this project.

E. Describe your firm's experience with Mechanical/Electrical trades and equipment. Please indicate how you propose to handle Mechanical/Electrical estimating.

F. Please enclose examples of the following from a previous project similar in size and scope to this project:
1. Schematic design phase estimate
2. Design development phase estimate
3. Construction document phase estimate
4. Project schedule
5. Interim report to the client

IV. Project Organization

Provide a project organization chart showing your key professionals who would be assigned to this project for both the preconstruction and construction phases. For each key professional, please provide the following information

A. Percentage of involvement for each project phase:
1. Design development
2. Construction documents
3. Bidding
4. Construction

B. Provide a brief description of their responsibilities on the project and their role within the project team.

C. Provide detailed resumes of these key professionals, showing work experience and education.

V. Additional Information

A. Please describe what distinguishes your firm from others in the field. Please identify what makes your firm a good candidate for this project.

B. Include a corporate brochure or other materials to supplement your firm's written qualifications.

VI. Fees and Reimbursable Expenses

A. The proposed Construction Management fees and proposed allowance for reimbursable expenses should be submitted in a separate, sealed envelope using Form B of this Request for Qualifications. The envelope should be identified with the name of this project and the name of your company.

B. The above fees should include all personnel time anticipated for all phases of the project, including the project manager, estimators, and clerical but not including the field representative. The field representative's time should be listed in the proposed allowance for reimbursable expenses.

C. Provide proposed allowances for reimbursable expenses (General Conditions including a detailed list with an anticipated dollar amount for each line item and a total for the entire project).

FORM A

Request for Proposal for Construction Management Services

Please complete this form and attach it to your proposal.

The full name of our firm is

_____
Name

_____
Address

_____
City   State   Zip Code

_____
Office Phone No.   Fax No.   Cell/Mobile No.

_____
Contact Person

Our firm has performance bond capabilities of:_____

Our firm carries liability insurance in the amount of:_____

Our firm carries Errors and
Omission Insurance in the
amount of:_____

The successful construction management firm will *not* be considered as a trade contractor or subcontractor for any of the proposed construction/renovations.

We have read and we understand the RFP as presented. We agree to comply with Roosevelt Library District's Policy and the (Yourstate) Human Rights Act related to sexual harassment. If chosen as a semifinalist, we agree that the Roosevelt Library District may conduct any investigation it deems appropriate to check on our previous projects. My signature represents compliance and understanding of this RFP.

_____
Signature and Title

FORM B

This form should be submitted in a separate, sealed envelope identified with the name of this project and the name of your company.

_____

Name of Firm   Contact Person/Phone No.

Please list the categories and final price for items that you identify as *pre-referendum services.*

$ _____
(Monetary total for pre-referendum services)

Please list the categories and total price for items that you identify as *preconstruction services* including bidding/contract award phase work.

$ _____
(Monetary total for preconstruction costs)

Please fill in your proposed professional fee as a percentage of actual construction costs (construction and postconstruction phases)

_____
(% of construction costs)

Please provide a lump sum price for items you identify as General Conditions for all construction phases: addition, renovations, and improvements. List the categories and give a price breakdown on an attached sheet.

$ _____
(Monetary total for General Conditions)

_____

Signature

_____

Title

_____

Date

Appendix C

Sample Advertisement for Bids

For most public projects, an Advertisement for Bids must be printed in one or more newspapers. This is a common format for an Advertisement for Bids.

Advertisement for Bids
Roosevelt Library District

Project Name and Location
A New Library for the Roosevelt Library District, 429 Augusta Ave., Yourtown, Yourstate

Give the official name of your project as well as its location.

Owner
The Roosevelt Library District, 1928 Hoover Place, Yourtown, Yourstate

Indicate the name of the public body responsible for the project and the address to which correspondence should be directed.

Architect
BCA, Elgin, Illinois
847-695-5840

Give the name of the architectural firm responsible for the bidding documents, along with the phone number.

Project Description
This project is to construct a 75,000-square-foot, single-story library building . . . (*continue as appropriate*)

Continue with project specifics as required to summarize the project briefly. Keep it as short as possible to reduce the cost of the advertisement.

Documents
Bidding documents will be available at the office of the architect after 1:00 p.m., April 1, 2008.

Coordinate this with the architect.

Deposit
A refundable deposit of $100 will be required for each of the first three sets of documents issued to prospective bidders. Additional sets may be purchased for $100 each. Unused sets must be returned for refund within thirty calendar days after bidding.

Coordinate these requirements with the architect. Bidding sets cost the architect (and hence the client) a significant amount of money to reproduce and should not be given away too freely.

Bid Forms
Each bidder will be required to submit two original, signed copies of the bid forms contained in the bidding package.

Coordinate this with the architect.

Bid Security

A bid bond in the amount of 10% of the bid amount shall be included with the completed bid forms.

Consult the architect and the library's legal counsel regarding bid security amounts and restrictions.

Bids Due

Bids are due by 10:00 a.m. prevailing time on April 21, 2008. Bids will be received at the business office located in the library at 1928 Hoover Place, Yourtown, Yourstate. Late bids will be rejected.

Coordinate this with the architect to help ensure that adequate time is allotted for the bidding process.

Bid Opening

Bids will be publicly opened at the library business office at 11:00 a.m., prevailing time, April 21, 2008.

Bids are usually opened on a weekday during business hours. If your project is sizable, you may need to hold it in a room sufficient to accommodate a large number of people who have come to watch the opening.

Minimum Qualifications of Bidders

Bidders are required to meet specific minimum qualifications. Qualification information is contained in the bid package.

Consult the architect and the library's legal counsel regarding the legalities and desirability of prequalifying bidders.

Bonds

Performance and labor and material payment bonds will be required in the full amount of the contract sum. Bonds will be made payable to the Roosevelt Library District.

Consult the architect and the library's legal counsel regarding acceptable bond ratings and appropriate bond amounts.

Agreement

AIA Document A101, Standard Agreement between Owner and Contractor

Cite the contract being used, usually the standard AIA contract.

Contract Time

All work under this contract shall be substantially complete by June 1, 2010.

Consult the architect regarding the appropriate construction time for your building. The completion date will be determined by the particulars of your project.

Appendix D

Sample Punch List

Punch lists are prepared by the architect at substantial completion of a project. They identify items that are incomplete and must be completed prior to final completion.

Punch List

Date prepared: July 27, 2007

Contractor:
James Enterprises Ltd., 50 E. Newer Ave., Yourtown, Yourstate

Project:
New library for the Roosevelt Library District, 429 Augusta Ave.

Contract No. 93-0454-81 Contract

Work: General

The following is a list of items to be completed or corrected by the contractor. Failure to include any item on this list does not relieve the contractor of his or her responsibility to complete all work in accordance with the contract documents.

Item No.	Location	Description of Completion or Correction
1.	Lobby (Room 101), door #1	Provide pull on north door.
2.	Lobby (Room 101), door #1	Touch up paint on door and paint exterior and interior door frame.
3.	Lobby (Room 101)	Coat racks were not installed.
4.	Lobby (Room 101)	Miniblinds were not installed.
5.	Lobby (Room 101)	The wall angle of the ceiling grid in all the rooms is not flush with the wall. This is causing the tiles to be raised. The angle needs to be adjusted.
6.	Lobby (Room 101)	Repair wood crown above door #1.
7.	Lobby (Room 101)	Install all shelves in the cabinets.
8.	Lobby (Room 101)	Provide flush bolt insert in concrete at north door.

9.	Exhibit Area (Room 102)	Provide flush entry mat. Trim mat to fit in opening.
10.	Exhibit Area (Room 102)	Remove paint on the louver in the ceiling.
11.	Exhibit Area (Room 102)	Repair wood crown mold above door #1.
12.	Exhibit Area (Room 102)	Caulk joint at 45 degree wall where the dry wall meets the concrete.
13.	Exhibit Area (Room 102)	Remove paint on thermostat.

Prepared by: BCA

Sample Program Summary

Forms like this can summarize data collected during the programming phase. Always review the program data to confirm that everyone has the same understanding of the program requirements.

Programming / Schematic Design
Roosevelt Public Library

Date: July 27, 2007

Room Name: Library Director's Office Suite

Room Location: Administration Area

Furniture / Equipment	Mechanical / Electrical	Architectural
Furniture One Desk Credenza 3 Chairs 1 File Cabinet Secretary/reception furniture similar but with typing return on desk and 3 additional file cabinets	**Heating / Vent. / AC** Provide zoned heating and cooling for individual room control	**Floors** Carpet
	Plumbing / Fixtures Not applicable	**Wall Partitions** Drywall
Equipment Not Applicable	**Communications** Networked Computer: Yes Telephone(s): Yes Other: Public address speaker in ceiling	**Ceilings** Material: Lay-in acoustical Height: 8'-0"
Hours of Operation 10:00 a.m. to 3:30 p.m.	**Electrical** Duplex outlets Recessed fluorescent fixtures with adequate illumination level for reading and writing	**Doors / Windows** Lockable, outward opening door with hold-open. No vision panel Provide window with view to river
Special Provisions		**Acoustical Requirements** Provide noise attenuation insulation to assure conversational privacy

Occupancy
Library Director
	Room Size
	Critical Dimensions:
	Administrator's Office:
	    12' x 15'
	Secretary / Receptionist:
	    12' x 12'
	Total required area: 324 sq. ft.
		Natural Lighting
		North window if possible

Additional Information:

Suite should be located in administration area and provide for easy access by staff and patrons.

Suite must be adjacent to business manager's office.

Provide coat closet.

Entry to office should be controlled by secretary/receptionist.

Provide wall space and accent lighting for 4'-0" wide x 5'-0" high framed photograph of library director.

Sample Proposed Scope of Work

This proposed scope of work can form the basis for an RFQ for an owner's representative.

Proposed Scope of Work for an Owner's Representative
Roosevelt Library District

PREDESIGN PHASE

Attend selected project meetings and coordinate Library relations with other government entities and utility companies.

DESIGN PHASE

Attend selected project meetings and coordinate Library relations with other government entities and utility companies.

Work with Architect to provide recommendations defining appropriate form of project delivery (Design-Bid-Build, Construction Management, etc.).

Secure approvals by regulatory agencies where required.

Review cost estimates with Architect.

BID AND AWARD PHASE

Assist Architect with prequalification of potential bidders (if appropriate).

File required notices and advertisements for bidding.

Attend prebid conference with Architect.

Review addenda to bids.

Attend bid opening and assist Architect with recommendation of appropriate bidder.

Attend postbid conference.

Attend preconstruction conference with Architect.

Review required permits and insurance coverage recommendations.

Review Contractor's construction schedule review with respect to Owner's schedule.

CONSTRUCTION PHASE

Attend project meetings with Architect and Contractor.

Review progress payment.

Attend Board meetings and provide reports on progress and schedule.

Review change order requests and approve on Owner's behalf.

POSTCONSTRUCTION PHASE

Assist Architect with reviews of status of substantial completion.

Assist Architect with certification of final completion.

Assemble maintenance and operations manuals.

Assist Contractor with securing permit for building occupancy.

Bibliography

American Institute of Architects. *The Architect's Handbook of Professional Practice.* Washington, DC: AIA, 1993.

———. *Selecting Architects for Public Projects.* Washington, DC: AIA, 1982.

American Institute of Architects and Consulting Engineers Council of Illinois. *Qualifications-Based Selection.* Chicago: AIA Illinois and CECI Illinois, 1993.

Batko, Anthony J., and Richard Thompson. *Building a New Library.* Chicago: Illinois Library Association, 1989. Part of the Trustee Facts File.

Coxe, Weld, et al. "Charting Your Course." *Architectural Technology,* May/June 1986, 52–58.

Dahlgren, Anders. *Planning the Small Public Library Building.* Chicago: American Library Association, 1985. No. 11 in the Small Libraries Publications series, this 24-page handbook summarizes basic steps in preparing for a building project.

Dailey, Kazuko. *Library Buildings Consultant List.* Chicago: American Library Association, 1993. Provides the names, addresses, and special experience offered by library building consultants.

Finn, Richard, and James R. Johnston. *Selecting Library Consultants.* Chicago: Illinois Library Association, 1989. Part of the Trustee Facts File.

Illinois House of Representatives. Illinois Public Act 87-673; An Act concerning Procurement of Architectural, Engineering, and Land Surveying Services by the State of Illinois. Springfield: State of Illinois, 1987.

Illinois Library Association, Public Library Section. *Avenues to Excellence II: Standards for Public Library Service in Illinois 1989.* Chicago: ILA, 1989.

Kuster, Larry D., and Rendi Mann-Stadt. "Selecting Professional Services and Local Government Liability." *AIA Illinois News,* Summer 1993, 2, 11.

Maister, David. *Managing the Professional Service Firm.* New York: Free Press, 1994.

Means Building Construction Cost Data, various editions. Norcross, GA: Reed Construction Data.

Natale, Joe, ed. "Special Construction Considerations." *Illinois Libraries,* December 1991, 617–636.

Palmer, Michey A. *The Architect's Guide to Facility Planning.* Washington, DC: American Institute of Architects and Architectural Record Books, 1981.

Pena, William, William Caudill, and John Focke. *Problem Seeking.* New York: Cahners Books International, 1977.

Professional Engineers in Private Practice. *Questions and Answers on the Procurement of A/E Services by Public Owners.* Alexandria, VA: National Society of Professional Engineers, n.d.

U.S. Green Buildings Council. *LEED Reference Guide for New Construction and Major Renovations (LEED NC)* Version 2.1, 2nd ed. Washington, DC: USGBC, 2003.

Index

Richard C. McCarthy, AIA, is a principal architect with Burnidge Cassell Associates, where he serves as project manager and library team leader. He has built, remodeled, and renovated numerous libraries. He is a popular speaker on library building and renovation issues at ALA, PLA, and state library association conferences. He serves on the Board of Trustees of the Gail Borden Library in Elgin, Illinois, and led a successful campaign for a $28 million building referendum.